ITALY

FROM THE AIR

To Jack and Martha

Merry Christmas

1993

Guido Alberto Rossi dedicates this book to Gisela
Franco and Stefano Lefèvre dedicate this book to Litty

"The charm of Italy is akin to that of falling passionately in love."
Stendhal

The authors and the publishers express their thanks to
Massimo Moriggi, Giuseppe di Chiara,
Enzo Bianchini, and Giancarlo Costa.

Translated from the French edition by
Daniel Wheeler

© 1992 Éditions Didier Millet, Paris.
First published in English in the United States of America by
The Vendome Press, 515 Madison Avenue, New York, N.Y. 10022.
Distributed in the United States of America by Rizzoli International Publications,
300 Park Avenue South, New York, N.Y. 10010.

Library of Congress Cataloging-in-Publication Data
Rossi, Guido Alberto, 1949-
[Italie vue du ciel, English]
Italy From The Air / text by Franco Lefèvre : photographs by Guido Alberto Rossi.
p. cm.
ISBN 0-86565-140-X
1. Italy—Pictorial works. 2. Italy—Aerial photographs.
I. Lefèvre, Franco. 1926- . II. Title.
DG420.R6613 1993
914.5'0022'2—dc20   93-12461 CIP

Printed and bound in Singapore.

ITALY

FROM THE AIR

FRANCO LEFEVRE

PHOTOGRAPHS BY GUIDO ALBERTO ROSSI

THE VENDOME PRESS

CONTENTS

The agricultural census of 1990 revealed that Italy has a total of 22,651,401 hectares (54,589,876 acres) of land under cultivation. PAGES 4–5: A mystical light radiates from the lonely chapel, a survivor of some unknown disaster, or perhaps merely worn down by time. Umbria cultivates sweetness and serenity, virtues inherited from Saint Francis of Assisi. PAGES 6–7: Garfagnana. A love of mimicry seems to have overcome the builders of this Tuscan town whose triangular plan mirrors the form of the mountain upon which it perches. PAGES 8–9: The Umbrian landscape. Harmony reigns between the relics of the past and the developments of recent times. PAGES 10–11: Assisi. In Saint Francis' home town, art has taken its inspiration primarily from religion.

EXHAVSTO SINV MARIS SPINVLORVM ET CALVORVM PONTES ALLVENTIS IAMQVE
TERRA IN OCTO PALMORVM ALTITVDINE EG ESTA ENDE REPENTE SVBVT VS
SPINVLORVM PONTEM AQVA INFLVENS FOSSAM OBVNDAVIT VNDE NICOLAVS
SFRRA DOMINCVS IDE TVRR E OANNES BAPTA AVRIA IVLIVS DE RVVERE ET
O FRANCIVS TINIANVS ET POST EVM HIER DE ECCLESIAT PATRES COMVNIS
PORTVS QVE CERVATORES PONTEM PRAEDICTVM VALLARI AGRVRSVS AQVAM
EXHAVRIRI MANDARVNT VT EVM A MARIS IMPETV PERRVPTVM RESTAVRAENT
OPVSQVE COEPTVM PERFICERENT· CVIOPERI ASSIDVE INTERFVERVNT
SVMMA CVM DILIGENTIA OMNIA FIERI CVRANTES ANNO 1597 PRIDIE IIDVS
IVLII AD XII KLEN: DECEM POST EEO MONENTES VT SIQVADO ALIAM IN
ALIQVA PORTVS PARTE PVRGATIONEM FIERI CONTIGERIT PONTES
MINIME FONDIANT NEC AD IPSOS SPATIO VICINTI PALMORVM ACCEDANT

Photographed from the air, Italy discloses at every click of the shutter a unique moment in her biography, a rich and complex history intermingled with an extremely diverse natural environment. In response to the close scrutiny of a historian and a geographer, as well as to the keen eye of a gifted photographer, Italy yields up two aspects of her character at once—the apparent and the secret—without ever revealing all. This book attempts to cover the full range of Italy's 301,000 square kilometers, a land whose geographical outline already existed twenty-three centuries ago. Along her interior as well as exterior frontiers, Italy—the bard of her own epic—answers to an echoing past, at the same time as she carries on a dialogue with the ancient peoples who gave her life. The first group to enter the scene are the Ligures and the Veneti in the northern part of the territory, the former to the west, the latter to the east. Farther down, from Emilia and Tuscany to Lazio and Campania, the Etruscans make their appearance in the 7th century B.C., following their voyage across the Mediterranean from distant Lydia. The origin of the Etruscans, who called themselves "people of Rosenna," remains a matter of dispute even today. Certain historians believe them to have come from Central Asia and others from the region of the Danube, while some authorities label them "the sons of mysterious Atlantis." One thing certain is that the Etruscans had a fundamental and enduring effect on Italian culture. Scholars and the merely curious arrive in legion numbers—sometimes from the ends of the earth—to visit ancient sites named Spina, Fiesole, Populonia, Vetulonia, Arezzo, Siena, Cortona, Chiusi, Tarquinia, Cerveteri, and Vulci, all of which harbor the vestiges of the brilliant and complicated Etruscan civilization, an inexhaustible world that, for five centuries, populated one-fifth of Italy. Even today further evidence of their habitats, customs, and costumes, their necropolises and arts may come to light, despite the proliferation of *tomboroli*—tomb robbers—whose spoils, especially those from such sites as Cerveteri and Spina, disappear daily to enrich the holdings of European and American collectors.

The Etruscans had to contend with the Romans throughout the centuries of their control over lands facing the Tyrrhenian Sea, from Campania to northern Tuscany, and, to a lesser degree, over the northern ones facing the Adriatic. Nevertheless, they had a considerable influence on their adversaries, stamping Roman civilization with their distinctive culture and way of life, from their worship of the humanities to the introduction of new crops, as well as new tools and techniques to facilitate working in the fields. Thanks to the Etruscans, it is said, the peoples of Italy began during this period to evince an extremely valuable trait of the Roman or, later, Italian character—the ability to progress by competing with neighboring peoples in whatever way these seemed to be superior. Montesquieu, in his *Deliberations on the Causes of the Grandeur of the Romans and Their Decadence*, analyzed how the Romans forged their identity in combat, deriving from armed strife the theory of means and objectives: "The Romans, believing themselves destined for war, and regarding it as the only art, committed their entire spirit and their every thought to perfecting war. It is no doubt a god, wrote Vegestius, who gave the Romans the idea of the legion.

PRECEDING PAGES: Genoa in the era of its splendor, portrayed in a 16th-century engraving. The city acquires a new look, thanks to the opening of the Via Aurea, essential to urban redevelopment. After expanding its commercial ties in Europe and the Orient, Genoa deservedly came to be known as "the Superb."

RIGHT: A panoramic view of Naples in 1875. This was a time when the contradictions peculiar to the "capital of the South" were multiplying. The city's upper middle class concerned themselves less and less with the fate of the masses. In the poorer quarters, the population reached a density of 100,000 inhabitants per square kilometer. BELOW: The River Po flowing through Turin in 1880. While rowers skim along the surface of the water, sand dealers scoop their commodity from the river banks, and laundresses rub away at huge bundles of linen and sheets.

They wanted the legion to comprise, at its core, a light regiment that could quickly engage in battle and, should the need arise, give ground. Legionaires were trained to move in military step—that is, to cover 20, and sometimes 24, miles in 5 hours. During these marches, they had to pack some 60 pounds. They were made to proceed at the double and to be ready to spring fully armed."

Naples in 1865. An overall view of the Carmelite Church of Castelnuovo, together with the port and the Via del Piliero. This street, now disappeared, once linked the Piazza Municipio to the Via Marina.

Following the Etruscans, the Latins and the Samnites also had to endure the humiliation of surrender, as did even the Italiot Greeks who, beginning in the 8th century B.C., had brought to the peninsula the incomparable seeds of philosophy, science, and art. The Romans initiated their most prodigious expedition when, in the 3rd century B.C., they penetrated the wealthy territories annexed by Magna Graecia. Here they found a new cultural identity, which for centuries would be continuously enriched by the Greek colonies. Xenophon summed it up thus: "Better our wisdom than the physical prowess of men and horses. It is not good to value power in place of beneficent wisdom. Indeed, should a people find in their midst an adroit pugilist, the good order of the town will derive no advantage from it." The Greek philosopher evidently hoped to persuade the warrior Romans that they must undergo a profound transformation, the better to throw their encumbering swords away for the sake of discovering the pleasures of the spirit. Moreover, they should foster good relations between neighboring peoples through the spread of writing, which would no longer be the privilege of a small and powerful minority. Xenophon offered the Romans a set of principles for revolutionary social change, which the Hellenist J.P. Vermont characterized in these terms: "Writing should become common among the citizenry and laws should be written. Only in this way would [laws] become truly the responsibility of all. If writing allows everyone to see what remains more or less hidden in Oriental civilizations, the rules of the political game—that is, free debate and contradictory argument—will also become the rules of the intellectual game. Like political matters, all the knowledge, discoveries, and theory that philosophers have drawn from nature will become common to the people at large."

Rome never abandoned its policy of assimilating the customs and cultures of conquered peoples. Thus, Etruscan humanism, Greek science, and the accumulated learning of all the federated peoples of the peninsula fused in the Roman crucible, where knowledge of every kind would be valued beyond measure. From this matrix, philosophers, mathematicians, architects, and the surveyors of the Capitol drew lessons needed for the transformation of the nation. New knowledge and know-how revived city and countryside alike, which took on a new aspect and skillfully applied the techniques and methods discovered elsewhere. Economy and trade assumed primary importance, at least until the Imperial

RIGHT: Naples in 1875. On the wide Via Marini, horse-drawn carriages, symbols of the wealthy bourgeoisie and the Neapolitan aristocracy, roll alongside the simple carts of country folk. On the right appears the now-vanished Villa del Popolo and its gardens planted with palm and tamarisk trees. BELOW: A panoramic view, from 1855, of the Piazza del Campo in Siena. Twice a year for more than seven centuries, on 2 July and 16 August, Siena stages the *corsa al Palio*, during which the city's seventeen *contrade* are represented by horses and their daring riders in a thrilling race around the square.

The Palazzo or Villa Farnese, a majestic pentagonal edifice built in the 16th century on the Caprarola Hill, was the work of the innovative architect Giacomo da Vignola. This master devised ornamental solutions to the difficulties presented by a circular courtyard, as well as by the stairs, which linked the two different rectangular gardens laid out in front of the palace.

era, when the system broke down under the unchecked financial power of the nouveaux riches and the military. The urbanization of the rural masses would also have its effect, especially in the central and southern parts of the peninsula. The contradictions between the uncontrolled growth of cities and a retreating countryside were further leading indicators of a political system in crisis.

In 602, Pope Gregory the Great complained: "Henceforth will anything agreeable be left in the world? The cities have been destroyed, the fortified sites ruined, the countryside depopulated, and the land reduced to wilderness." More than four centuries had passed since the Tiber—a few hundred meters from the Roman Forum, just below the gilded villas on the Aventine Hill where the powerful lived—saw ships dock at a frenetic rate in order to satisfy the unslakable thirst of an affluent society—for rare marbles, precious and fragrant woods, obelisks, colossal statues, multicolored mosaics. Rome was adorning herself with temples—some twenty-eight of them—baths, and pharaonic villas. Overriding the linear and well-ordered traces of her first establishments, the Imperial city commenced, with total abandon, to imitate the legendary capitals of the Middle East. Meanwhile, the number of her inhabitants grew to more than a million.

The archaeological vestiges at the center of historic Rome—so perfectly picked out by aerial photography—are the melancholy residue of an architectural ensemble from the time of the Emperors Augustus, Claudius, Hadrian, and Trajan. "I found a city of brick, I leave it a city of marble," said Augustus, the proud reformer. Here lie fallen a stone head, a pair of feet, a hand, all of marble and gigantic; there a mutilated equestrian statue, fragments of Doric, Ionic, or Corinthian capitals in the thousands, piled up in the gardens bordering the Forum, or set into the walls of churches and public buildings. This heap of scraps bears witness to the passage of invaders—the Alaric Goths and their rivals—as well as to the pillages wrought upon the ancient capital city during subsequent centuries, with the assent of those master predators, Rome's patricians and popes.

With the decline of the Western Empire began the stratification of various cultures brought to different parts of the peninsula by conquerors eager to establish themselves on lands formerly unified under the sons of Romulus. Everywhere, moreover, rose the places of Christian worship, finally out of the catacombs. Often their foundations would be the ruins of the pagan temples that had preceded them. This architectural metamorphosis, which was especially marked in the Middle Ages, led Christian dignitaries into unforeseen competition with resurgent secular powers. Frequently the barons seized former Imperial monuments in order to construct fortified houses. Thus, even today one can discover in the higgledy-piggledy lanes of historic Rome the jutting form of a former nobleman's tower attached to the façade of a church, which, in a still more remote time, had been a temple.

Other Italian cities, like the ancient capital, suffered a decline made worse by bloody and ceaseless internal strife. In Ravenna, Naples, and Milan, the antagonists were primarily the Byzantines and the Lombards. Equally determined to retain the loyalty of all the territory's diverse peoples, both parties took up positions at strategic locations from which they would long dominate their respective domains. The ruins of these impregnable strongholds stud the terrain of Lazio, Umbria, and Meridional or Southern Italy. During later periods they would serve as the prototypes of fortresses that even today bedeck the Italian landscape, all together providing an incomparable range of architectural styles and means, from the austere *rocca* perched upon a sheer peak to the castle/villa no longer equal to the military functions of the fortified outposts the Romans called *castellae*. The inventory, which is enormous, includes the ruins of Graines in the Val d'Aosta, Montalto with its impressive defenses, Castel del Monte in Apulia, Castel del Buon Consiglio at Trent, Pavia, the Gradara *rocca*, Vignola, the gigantic Villa Farnese at Caprarola, Sasso di Montefeltro, the Sant'Andrea fort, Ferrara's magnificent fortified castle, and the Palazzo Ducale at Urbino.

From the air, we can enjoy discovering houses flanked by medieval towers in the Trentino, only to encounter soon thereafter, among cypresses and olive trees, the sophisticated variations on the theme developed during the Renaissance—the villas of the Medici in the Florentine countryside, civilized places rich in decorative effects and gardens. Beyond the architectural splendors, deep within the shadows of history, we can only imagine the obscure life of illiterate peasants devoid of power, as well as that of the minor clergy and craftsmen with their legendary skills. Artists of genius would never have succeeded, nor would their talent have been fulfilled, without the collaboration of anonymous individuals: stone cutters, engravers, gilders, simple laborers, and apprentices, whose faces and signatures are lost forever. Art, artisan, artist, work of art—all are interlinked and indispensable. Leonardo Sciascia, in a book whose title translates as *Italy of the Ex-capitals*, has quite justly

Rome, 1890. Saint Peter's Basilica and the buildings on the former Prati di Castello, which a few years earlier had been given over to kitchen gardens, cane fields, and groves of trees. The photograph offers a glimpse of the new urban plan for Rome, close to the gridded order of Turin.

called attention to that fecund and vital alliance. Indeed, great vitality surged right through the country, a land of infinite virtues as well as abundant faults, but nonetheless the product of more than a millennium of interwoven traditions and cultures brought by Mediterranean and Nordic peoples from both the East and the West. These different ethnic groups lived side by side within the same territory, albeit in a perpetual state of reciprocal wariness. Frequently, they also failed to understand one another and thus caused mutual grief. They suffered through centuries of history that saw power alternately shift from one group to the next, totally indifferent to the ongoing or the future. The rare exceptions arise less from the structures of daily life than from continuity with the past manifested in a fresh reordering of the public domain. At Lucca, for example, the elliptical marketplace as we know it today corresponds exactly to the plan of a one-time Roman amphitheater, just as in Rome the plan of the Piazza Navona follows that of the circus built under the Emperor Domitian. The architects Bernardo Rossellini and Luciano Laurana reconceived the genesis of the urban center as a series of "ideal cities" that far surpassed the urban projects of a metropolis like contemporary Rome. Financed by Pope Pius II, Rossellini undertook in 1459 to remodel the old city of Corsignano, which belonged to the Tuscan pontiff. On the piazza he sited the city's central hub—the cathedral—which served as a backdrop framed by two different palaces—the Piccolomini (Pius II's family name) and the Episcopal. Several decades later, according to some art historians, Michelangelo remembered this composition when he remodeled the Piazza del Campidoglio in Rome. In 1468, Laurana began work on the Palazzo Ducale in Urbino, the property of Federigo da Montefeltro. Giulio Carlo Argan and Maurizio Fagiolo, in their book entitled *I caratteri originali della storia d'Italia*, wrote that, throughout this ducal palace, Laurana "gives form to a Humanist idea—a military architecture transformed into a civil architecture. The façade turned towards the valley recalls French châteaux of the Late Gothic period; cliff, tower, and walls are typical fortifications, even though reduced in size and refined, as would be tournament armor in contrast to combat armor." Baldassare Castiglione got it right when he characterized the ensemble of structures at Urbino as "a city in the form of a palace."

The rebirth of man and of primary values abandoned for centuries, hymns to the new dignity of the arts and letters—such was the meaning of the issues that Humanists, from every part of the Italy, addressed to both the Church and their rich patrons. Thus, we find Lorenzo Ghiberti speaking of "Byzantine brutalities," while Brunelleschi dismissed Gothic buildings as "cursed constructions that have made the world drunk." According to the critic Francesco De Sanctis, Machiavelli acted as "the conscience and thought of the country, of a society that looked inside, interrogated, and knew itself. Machiavelli is the Italian Luther, the implacable critic of that feeble Italy, corrupt and overly devoted to the cult of form."

Rereading Vitruvius, the ancient and peerless technician, helps us to understand the new concepts of equilibrium and proportion whereby the architecture of urban communities, with their radial zones and streets converging towards the center, would be founded upon the principle of regularity. In the work of the two Sangallos, Baldassare Peruzzi, Andrea Palladio, and Leonardo da Vinci, such

A plan of Padua in a 17th-century engraving. The mighty fortifications that surround the urban settlement, including the suburbs, had been constructed in the 16th century by the Venetians. The strategic position of Padua, at the far inland boundary of the lagoon Republic, required that the defenses be virtually impregnable.

concepts become almost reality. Then, following the great "functionalist" lesson given by Leon Battista Alberti, the 16th century, by creating a harmony of man and his city, left its indelible mark upon the history of architecture.

Turin, 1902. The little train that crossed the Piazza Castello was a touristic wonder at the time. The meandering railway was even used for the daily delivery of fresh milk. "A souvenir photo of the tender archaeology of yesteryear," commented the writer Luciana Frassati, author of *Torino come era*.

In Rome, Turin, Naples, Venice, Milan, and, most of all, Florence, the discourse of the Renaissance unfolded. Italy still marvels at the exuberance of the monuments inspired by Renaissance aesthetics. Indeed, the nation is even prouder of this achievement than of the Baroque or the Neoclassical, which nonetheless brought abundant and exquisite graces to many Italian cities, churches, and villas. Artists such as Bramante, Leonardo da Vinci, Luca Signorelli (a disciple of Piero della Francesca), Andrea del Sarto, Piero di Cosimo, Giovanni and Gentile Bellini, Carpaccio, Titian, Lorenzo Lotto, Giorgione, Correggio, Bernardo Luini, Michelangelo, and Raphael shared the big leading roles so that the people, and not solely the society that ordered and financed it, might enjoy the performance. A letter written by Raphael gives us an insight into the artistic process at its very inception. "In order to paint Adam," he wrote, "it would be necessary to have Michelangelo do the drawing, leave the coloring to Titian, and from Raphael take the proportions and the appropriate expressions." This ideal discloses an authentically Italian formula: team play. But the game produces superior results only after the most intense competition, an exchange fraught with rival ideas and a long evolution in the face of contradictions that at first appeared irreconcilable. The astonishing variety of Latin temperaments, rich in history, explains the incredible capacity of Southerners to preserve their ebullience even after they emigrate to the dull geometry of factories along the Po Valley. It also explains the versatility and optimism of the "computer men" of the North who settle in the South, bringing with them their enterprise and their families. How different they are from the Italians of 1740 as described by France's Président de Brosse: "Imagine a people composed of one-third priests, one-quarter statues, one-third who do not work at all, and the other third who count for nothing. . . ."

Whether from the North, the Center, or the Mezzogiorno (South), the Italians of today have surely assimilated, even if unconsciously, a *modus operandi* as old as the Italian soil, which is to elbow through the crowd at the first opportunity: "Here, only the nature that surrounds you will teach you the secret of survival. Here, with each new season, you must reinvent yourself."

The photographs in this work capture the slow-moving history of Italy, the history of men, of nature, and of monuments from the past, sometimes too the image of a more burning history, of an overflowing vitality, the history of an Italy that, at the end of the 20th century, is absolutely astounding in her dynamism.

URBINO.

URBINO.

S. Maria della tomba
Tempio anticuss d'Ouidis

SVLMO OVIDII
PATRIA.

This engraving represents Urbino in the Marche. Jewel of the Renaissance, Urbino has preserved its imposing ramparts, which reflect the transition from the time of the Romans to that of the Montefeltro family. Luciano Laurana, who in 1466 took charge of construction work on the Palazzo Ducale, unified old Gothic structures with the new ideas of the Renaissance. This masterpiece of harmony looms menacingly above a steep cliff.

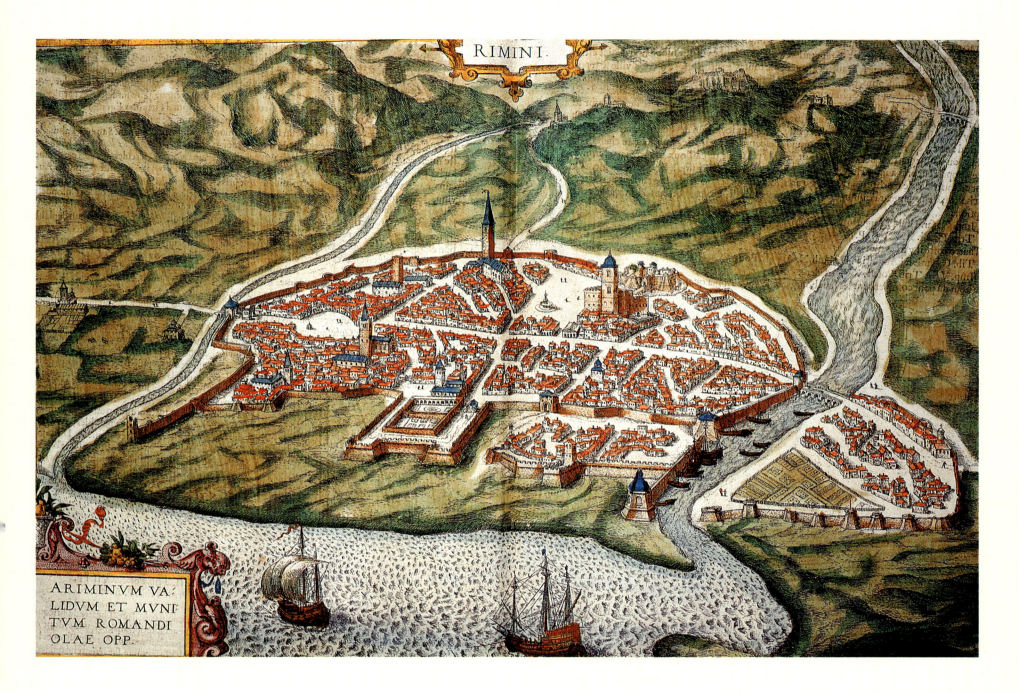

RIMINI.

ARIMINVM VA:
LIDVM ET MVNI·
TVM ROMANDI
OLAE OPP.

An engraving of Rimini. The austerity suggested by this old plan contrasts with the atmosphere of the modern city, now a lively seaside resort. In the engraving, Rimini retains traces of the Roman occupation, when the town was known as Ariminum: the five-arch bridge of Tiberius and the Arch of Augustus. It was in the 15th century, during the reign of Sigismondo Malatesta, that Rimini reached the summit of its power and splendor.

NORTHERN ITALY

The mountain barrier that forms Italy's northern limits has ceased to be regarded as a defensive rampart. This change of attitude, which some call a regeneration, has come about only recently. The almost continuous Alpine chain—situated like a head crowning a long body elsewhere immersed in the Mediterranean—no longer functions as a separation between countries but instead provides a complement to them. The product of inter-European dialogue, this new reality commenced in 1871, the year that saw the completion of the huge Fréjus railway tunnel linking France and Italy. During the next thirty-five years, two other vital openings were pierced in the Alpine wall—the Saint-Gothard in 1882 and the Simplon in 1906. The Great-Saint-Bernard Tunnel, completed in 1964, was built for automobile traffic, as was the Mont-Blanc Tunnel. This facility, inaugurated in 1965, now makes it possible to pass right through Europe's highest mountain mass in a quarter of an hour. The unification project affects not only Italians in the North but also those of the entire peninsula, and, thanks to these open doors, age-old economic isolation and cultural insularity have both come to an end.

The accounts of Alpine voyages left by 18th-century writers have an epic tone about them. In those days it was a brave and daring feat to cross the mountains into Italy, an enterprise comparable to those undertaken by the armies of Charlemagne and Frederick Barbarossa. In 1713, the Anglo-Irish philosopher George Berkeley wrote of risking his life every step of the way over and down Mount Cenis, which he deemed one of the most "terrifying and inaccessible" massifs in the whole of the Alps. Nearly a century later, in 1810, Alphonse de Lamartine recalled his own descent towards Turin over the peaks and slopes of Mount Cenis, where he "felt himself passing through the gates to the old world." Frightened no doubt by such dramatic descriptions, some famous travelers scratched the redoubtable Alps from their itineraries and took the alternative route by sea. Thus, Président de Brosse left his native Dijon and arrived in 1839 by way of the Saône, the Rhône, and the Mediterranean, having managed at Marseilles to embark on a felucca bound for Genoa. The Ligurian coast that greeted the Bourguignon dignitary in the early 18th century was scarcely the one familiar today, crushed as this is under massive construction and run through by a network of tortuous highways. Once landed at Genoa, "the Superb," de Brosse believed ". . . one could say, with a measure of truth, that Genoa is entirely painted in fresco. The streets are nothing more than enormous stage sets for opera."

The description remains valid even now despite the inroads of modernity. The Bianco, Rosso, Doria Tursi, and Spinola palaces, the University, the Cambiaso, the Parodi, the Cathedral of San Lorenzo, Sant'Ambrogio, the Royal and Ducal palaces bear splendid witness to

PRECEDING PAGES: Mount Baldo offers a magnificent view over Lake Garda.
LEFT: Mount Cervin, or Cervino, in the Val d'Aosta. Pyramidal in form and permanently snow-covered, Mount Cervin reaches an altitude of 4,478 meters. At the northwest extremity of the peninsula, it marks the frontier between Italy and Switzerland's Valais canton. The summit entered the history of alpinism when an intrepid team led by Edward Whymper conquered it on 14 July 1865.

Much favored by artists, the luxurious seaside resort of Portofino was originally a small fishing village nestled within the sheltering recess of a natural cove. The forests in the background serve as the "green lungs" of the Ligurian Riviera. From April to September, Portofino presents its attractions, beginning with the first regattas, which run their course in the spring. Autumn brings still further embellishment to the enchanted view of coves cradling limpid, jewel-toned water surrounded by olive trees, yews, and maritime pines.

The Mole Antonelliano is 167 meters in height. Its masonry construction, once the most advanced in Europe, was a great achievement for Italian architecture at the end of the 19th century. Still the emblem of Turin, the Mole was built for the Jewish community, who were eager to celebrate the closing of the ghettos in 1848. Today it is no longer crowned by the Star of David originally designed for the spire, but by a sword and palm leaf. Alessandro Antonelli, the Mole's bold architect, died without having ever seen the great monument completed. At the works site, we are told, he demanded that every brick weigh the same, since even a small variation risked creating imbalances that could have resulted in damage to the structure.

the refinement of Genoese architecture. Moreover, they all conceal pictorial masterpieces, some of them by such painters as Rubens, Antonello da Messina, Van Dyck, Bernardo Strozzi, Giovanni Pisano, and Gérard David. West and east, from San Remo to La Spezia, villages, small towns, and villas strive to upstage one another while playing second fiddle to the true high points of Liguria. Bay after bay, their multicolored jumble serves as a foil not only to treasures inherited from the past—the villages of San Fruttuso and Cinque Terre, as well as those in the hinterland of La Spezia—but also to grafts developed during the last twenty-five years, at Rapallo, Santa Margherita Ligure, Portofino, Camogli, and Bordighera. Savona, meanwhile, can justly boast of being Liguria's second port, thanks to the extent and modernity of its petrochemical installations and its maritime industry.

In this domain, Liguria can be readily compared with Piedmont next door, a territory conquered by the automobile princes. In 1899, Giovanni Agnelli abandoned his dream of inventing perpetual motion and kicked off the assembly-line production of motor cars. The region underwent profound physical change as the Piedmontese sought their fortune in the promises of industrialization. Perhaps it was here, in Turin's gigantic motor-car industry and its environment, that first came into being the phenomenon that Gillo Dorfles, a close observer of contemporary life, calls "temporal pollution"—the modification of our biological clock in the interest of mass manufacture. Dorfles urges a rapid return to time set or punctuated by the human body's own rhythm, "by the somewhat inexact clocks of yesteryear and not by the quartz ones of today, whose precision is intolerable."

However, many and recent indices confirm that at least one part of Piedmont has not followed the irresistible and devouring rise of the motor-car industry. Here and there, small- and medium-sized enterprises have revived in the hope of claiming their autonomy. They flourish most of all in viticulture, the mechanical arts, textiles, and chemicals. Still, the denizens of such "independent" cities as Ivrea, Alessandria, and Novara hold Turin, the provincial capital, in the kind of affectionate respect owed to a venerable parent. Of course, it would be very difficult not to revere a city that, according to Nietzsche, one should love for its "heretical clarity." The Torinese are happy to be thought austere, modest, and true to their word. They willingly cite the proud ancestral heritage of their world and its beauties. The layout of Turin, for example, adheres to the street plan originally traced out by the Romans, with its regular grid of intersecting streets. Viewed from the air, such ingenious discipline will delight surveyors, geometricians, architects, and urbanists enamored of Classicism. The architectural treasures of Turin include the Palazzo Carignano, built by the Baroque

View over the roofs of Milan. The massive bombardments carried out in August 1943 by the British and American air forces destroyed houses and factories erected since the beginning of the 19th century. Then came the great wave of immigration from the South, which added to the need for new construction. This time, the buildings would have from ten to twelve stories, thereby permanently changing the physical character of the Lombard city.

master Guarino Guarini, the Palazzo Madama, the Stupinigi hunting lodge erected by Filippo Juvarra, the bold and singular Mole Antonelliana. Equally notable are the collections in the Egyptian and Risorgimento museums.

Piedmont, for more than thirty years the protagonist, along with Lombardy and Liguria, of a powerful economic expansion, nonetheless clings tenaciously to the essential qualities of her nature. The province contains, for instance, fourteen natural parks. Further, safeguarding the ecology has become *de rigueur* in Piedmont, where protests against the uncontrolled barbarism of industrialization become ever more urgent. Like Milan, Turin is an egocentric metropolis, in whose whirlpool surrounding communities say they are being drowned. The phenomenon has had alarming ramifications in the suburbs, where old quarters and hamlets are little more than a memory of their former selves. Much too often proliferating urban projects aggress upon the once-unspoiled landscape. Such changes remind one of the famous rebukes uttered by John Kenneth Galbraith against the "unseemly economics of expansion" in the United States, where capitalism allowed private opulence to triumph in the midst of public poverty.

Elsewhere in Lombardy, the love of nature and the past remains deeply rooted. Italy's fourth largest region, Lombardy provides several dazzling variations on its most favored landscape themes: mountains, plains, lakes, and hills. One can easily identify with Chateaubriand when he writes: "My opinions underwent correction all across Lombardy, which takes a while to have its full effect upon the traveler. At first you see a very rich country on the whole, and you say: 'It's quite good.' But when you examine things more closely, the enchantment begins to take hold. Meadows whose verdure surpasses the freshness and trim of English lawns mingle with fields of corn, rice, and wheat, over which rise vines that hang from prop to prop, making garlands above the cereal crops. This scene could be found in forty different places, gathering riches all the way to Milan, the focal point of the picture. To the right appear the Apennines and to the left, the Alps." An admiring Alfredo Baccelli described the 5-kilometer-long Forni Glacier thus: "Essentially a diadem of clouds or snowy needles enveloped in a lunar veil—the crest of the Forno massif. They could have been slumbering giants."

From the cold of the névés to the mild climate of the lakes—Maggiore, Iseo, Como, Lugano, and Garda—fringed with lemon and olive trees, the change is radical. Shelley, who traversed the region about 170 years ago, evoked it in these terms: "The mountains between Como and that village [of Tremezzo], or rather cluster of villages, are covered on high with chestnut forests (the eating chestnuts, on which the inhabitants of the country subsist in time of scarcity), which sometimes descend to the very verge of the lake overhanging it with

In Lombardy, the River Ticino flows from its source in the Saint Gothard massif and then joins the Po downstream from Pavia. Once it leaves Lake Maggiore, the Ticino is exploited at various points along its course for irrigation purposes via a complicated network of canals.

Como, the eponymous capital of its province, is tucked away in a small cove at the extreme southwest end of a lake shaped like an inverted Y. Dominated by the Gauls, the Romans, who gave it a fleet of boats, the Milanese, the Visconti family, the Spanish, the Hapsburgs, the French under Napoleon, and then the Austrians, Como was finally liberated by Garibaldi in 1859. The town has now become a center of textile production, with the charming title of "silk capital" of Italy.

their hoary branches. But usually the immediate border of this shore is composed of laurel-trees, and bay, and myrtle, and wild fig trees, and olives which grow in the crevices of the rocks, and overhang the caverns, and shadow the deep glens, which are filled with the flashing light of the waterfalls." Needless to say, the scene painted by Shelley has subsequently endured far too many abuses. Still, hope springs eternal, and indeed, during the last forty years, the transgressions have ceased, thanks to enlightened measures taken by the government and the vigilance of environmentalists.

After nature and history comes prehistory. The adventure of men and women who lived on lands formerly called Longobardia could very well have begun at Capo di Ponte, a village situated in the Val Camonica, a few kilometers from Lake Iseo. There, for eight millennia, from the Stone Age to the Iron Age, a people called the Camuni carved some 180,000 figures on rocks forming an integral part of their habitat. This immense family album incised in stone constitutes the world's most imposing library, as the archaeologist Sabatini Mosati observed. The extraordinary authors of these memoirs have left an almost "photographic" record of their aesthetic evolution: scenes of hunting and then animal husbandry, religious vignettes in which a dog or occasionally a star is worshipped, agricultural scenes animated by four-wheeled plows pulled by oxen, and illustrations of ritual dancing. A study of these carvings makes it possible to conclude that "an Alpine civilization [existed] earlier even than the all-important emergence of Mesopotamian and Neolithic civilizations." Experts believe that other discoveries may yet be made among the rocks of Capo di Ponte.

An old but much later and relatively well-preserved history of Lombardy unfolds in more than a hundred castles, scattered about the nine provinces of Sondrio, Como, Milan, Pavia, Mantua, Cremona, Brescia, Bergamo, and Varese. At Varese, on the edge of Lake Maggiore, looms up the Rocca d'Angera, which belonged successively to the Romans, the Longobards, and the Visconti family. Built of stone and red brick, these structures—some massive, others tall and slender—bear witness to the styles of military or civil life from 1100 to 1600. In addition, they contain art works of inestimable value, such as the "Bridle Chamber" in the Castello San Giorgio at Mantua with its frescoes painted by Andrea Mantegna.

The castle of the Sforzas in Milan during winter. An enormous brick quadrilateral, the fortress was built in the 15th century for Francesco Sforza. Although restored in the 19th century by Beltrami, it suffered extensive damage during the Second World War. The castle houses a rich complex of museums.

Thanks to castles, keeps, dungeons, fosses, armories, portraits, and nuptial chambers, reconstituting the history of great families brings to life the saga of the Lombards, a fascinating saga rich in mystery. The story seems all the more captivating for the imaginative alternative it presents to the uniformity of Milan, the pilot city, which however cannot be denied its preeminent role in the nation, a city capable of the sangfroid required for dealing with the rest of the world.

To judge from the lead given by Milan, it would seem that modernity

A mesmerizing puzzle in red brick! Thus presented, coiffed in tiles, Bologna hides its many faces. The Bolognese call their city *turrita*—bristling with towers. Bologna is also a center of learning and scholarship. Beginning in the 13th century, the local university, founded in 425, could boast some ten thousand students. The natural sciences held pride of place, with anatomy lessons using limewood models and even cadavers. Finally, Bologna is a "fat" city, meaning a place where one eats wonderfully well, on the best sausages and the tastiest pastas prepared *alla bolognese*, with a sauce of meat and tomatoes. The Emilian film director Pupi Avati "loves Bologna because it is at the center of the world without being part of it."

In this quarter at the center of historic Bologna cluster the oldest of the city's churches, aristocratic dwellings, and the few remaining medieval towers out of the original 180. It was here that the people of the Villanovan period, from the 11th to the 10th century B.C., set up their huts. Conquered by the Etruscans, who called the place Velzna, then by the Boïan Gauls (from Bohemia), Bologna became a Latin colony in 189 B.C., under the name *Bononia* ("settlement"). In 1088 came the founding of the first school in Western Europe for studies in Roman law. The School of Bologna experienced a great revival during the 12th and 13th centuries.

counts above all else, a reality most immediately evident in the city's brisk and efficient way of engaging in activities as diverse as they are rational. In 1962, the humorist Marcello Marchesi described the Milanese haste in this way: "I live in a city occupied by hyper-occupied people. They all walk rapidly and don't even look at women until after 9 o'clock in the evening. This city wakes up one minute earlier every day. She is already living through the month of January 1965. . . ." As for the second principle dear to the Milanese, an old proverb says it best: *A palanch a palanch se fa a rent cent franc* ("Soldo by soldo, that makes a hundred lire").

The people of Venice have no use for such frenzy. "Here, time passes one way or another," noted Carlo Bernari in *Italia dei grandi viaggiatori*. "As in every antique civilization, one may enjoy all the slow, attenuated moments provided one adapts to their rhythm. Here, time wastes more than it gains! And if you, a foreigner, succeed in matching your internal rhythms to the external rhythms of the city, you will not be surprised to catch yourself revisiting San Marco or the Accademia, taking a second or even a third look at a Titian, a Tintoretto, or a Palma Vecchio, returning to the Biblioteca Marciana to savor an old Latin or Greek manuscript. In the streets, galleries, and lanes, time always has time to lose in order to leave us enough so that, without being haunted by the fleeting hours, we can take pleasure in the most secret sense of the metaphysical that governs the real life of the city." The nature of the Venetians may have been given its truest definition by Goffredo Parise: "I asked myself what culture could join the solemn beauty of Palladian columns, of bricks and Paduan arcades, of Verona's bridges, of scintillating Venice . . . to the enormous quantity of small and large factories in the Veneto, and I found only one: the barbarian force of a land that until yesterday produced work in the fields and today produces work in factories. A barbarian force and not Latin or Mediterranean culture. In a certain sense, another invasion—that of industrial labor in place of agriculture."

South of the Veneto, Emilia owes her name to the Via Emilia, the long, straight Roman route that ran from Piacenza to Rimini. Benefiting from a communication axis essential to Central and Southern Italy as well as to the North, the Emilians have set aside the bitter memories of the age-old emigration to which Venetians are now subject. Like the

Romagnese—the people of the Romagna province—they have learned that in addition to getting the most for their crops and cattle, they must also invest agricultural profits in small- and medium-sized industries such as food products, clothing, shoes, and, finally, tourism. For some years now along the Adriatic coast, from Cattolica to Cervia, there has stretched the most luxurious tourist zone in all of Italy, where Ferrara, Ravenna, and Parma are just so many rest stops on the way to Paradise.

The track at Imola in Emilia-Romagna is an annual gathering place for Italians devoted to motor racing.

Four islands are found in Lake Garda: Sogno, Olivo, Trimelone, and Garda, the last facing the promontory of Portese. In the lush vegetation of the lake's enchanted shores, the monks of San Zeno built their retreat more than a thousand years ago. The choice of site, dictated by a desire to pursue their studies in tranquil surroundings, would be imitated five centuries later by the Friars Minor. Virgil, Goethe, and Gabriele D'Annunzio evoked Lake Garda under the name "Benacus" ("the Beneficent").

On Lake Garda, the medieval *rocca* or fortress of Sirmione, erected by the Scaligers in 1259, stands between the bay of Desenzano and that of Peschiera. Sirmione was restored in 1918 to its former glory in which Martino I della Scala had originally taken such boastful pride. With two fortified enceintes, one 30-meter tower, crenelated walls, four keeps, and a fortified harbor, the *rocca* is as famous as the Garda region's other masterpiece—the Roman villa known as the "Baths of Catullus."

The Borromean Isles of
Lake Maggiore. RIGHT:
In 1630, Count Carlo
Borromeo began
transforming what
would later be known
as the Isola Bella,
dedicated to his wife
Isabella, into a place
that would become the
delight of garden-lovers
as well as those
interested in the arts.
BELOW: The small Isola
dei Pescatori retains the
picturesque charm of a
fishing village, which it
formerly was.

In the Val d'Aosta, daily life reveals its several aspects. At the foot of Mont Blanc, and along a 100-kilometer stretch, traditional agriculture continues to be practiced alongside all manner of modern activities: tourist sports, the generation of hydroelectric power, steel and textile production. Characteristic of the area are houses roofed with slabs of flat stone known as Lauzes.

At Fenis, on the banks of the River Dora Baltea, a medieval fortress of the 14th century crowns a dominating site. Its courtyard is decorated with frescoes. The castle has undergone extensive restoration.

The fortress of Bard in the Val d'Aosta, over whose gorges Ottone dei Bard sought to achieve absolute control. About a thousand years ago, he ordered the construction of this formidable castle, one of the best examples of the defensive outposts scattered along the frontier with France.

More than a mountain barrier, the Alpine region tells a story of geological activity in the distant past, as calcareous towers, crystalline peaks, such as Mont Blanc at 4,807 meters, and morainic circuses and amphitheaters reveal the effects of glacial erosion. On the lower slopes of the massif, wherever the soil proved favorable, Indo-Europeans became the first human beings to venture this far north, soon followed by the Altaics, all sowing the seeds of the dialects still spoken in these Alpine valleys.

A close look at the rock faces of the Dolomite peaks reveals variations in the limestone, whose basic color is a deep pink called "dolomite." The jagged massif harbors traces of porphyry and quartz that arouse curiosity about what may be concealed within.
FOLLOWING PAGES: The Charterhouse of Pavia is one of the most remarkable monuments in all of Lombard art. Gian Galeazzo Visconti founded the monastery in 1396. However, it was in the 15th century that the architect Amadeo built the lower extension, after which Lombardo completed the structure during the next century. The plan of the charterhouse remains Late Gothic, but many Renaissance elements have been incorporated into the façade, unfinished but lavishly embellished with polychrome marble sculptures, statues, and a frieze of medallions. Two cloisters, one small and the other large, both decorated with terracottas, adjoin the magnificent church at the center of the complex.

Agriculture in Lombardy. In ancient times, and even in the period of the Longobard invasion, forests covered a good part of the Lombard plains. The present state of the land is the result of the kind of agrarian development that, since the 18th century, has become common among the inhabitants of these regions. Progressively, farmers have rationalized their production and combined to form cooperatives. By this means, small family operations have been transformed, creating villages with populations in the thousands.

The Basilica of Saint Ambrose, founded at the end of the 4th century by Ambrose, Bishop of Milan, is especially venerated by the Milanese. The saintly Bishop's sermons caused such wonder that a liqueur made from honey came to be known as "ambrosia," the symbol of holy eloquence. The illustrious prelate was again evoked in the name of Milan's celebrated library, the Biblioteca Ambrosiana, installed in a 17th-century palace. It houses a distinguished collection of rare manuscripts—one of them annotated by Petrarch—while the picture gallery contains masterpieces of Italian and Flemish painting.

The Piazza del Duomo, at the end of a vast esplanade, is dominated by the marble cathedral. Commenced in 1386 on the orders of Gian Galeazzo Visconti, then continued in the 15th and 16th centuries by Italian, French, and German masters, the edifice was finally completed in the 19th century. Here, one must take a walk on the roofs and marvel at the 135 Gothic spires and the countless statue-pinnacles.

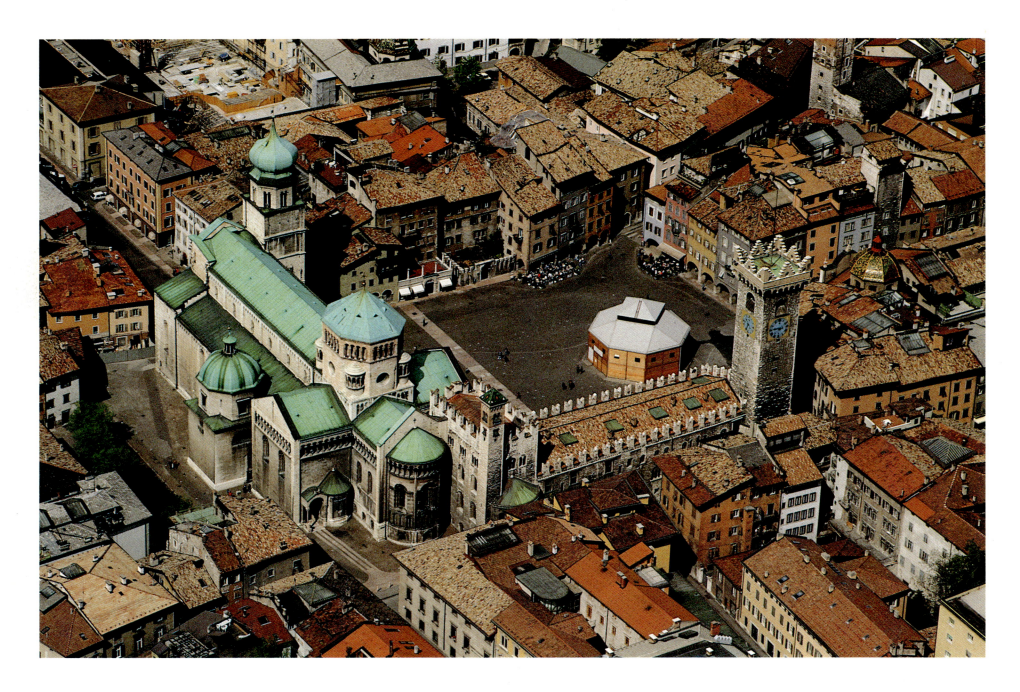

Trentino-Alto-Adige.
For 800 years, until the
19th century, Trent was
governed by prince-
bishops of the Holy
Roman Empire. Of all
the monuments in this
ancient city, the most
important is the
majestic cathedral,
whose foundation dates
from the 6th century.
Today, however, the
building impresses
mainly by virtue of the
13th-century
reconstructions carried
out by Adamo Arogno
in the Lombard
Gothic style.

Trieste—Tergeste under the Romans, an Austrian protectorate in 1382, and a free port in 1719—rejoined Italy only in 1954. Perched atop San Giusto Hill, the old city of Trieste is a tangle of narrow streets and elderly dwellings, all rich in history. The contrast with the neoclassical buildings of the modern city, grouped about the famous Piazza dell'Unità d'Italia, is arresting indeed.

Admirably situated at the water's edge, and facing both the Grand Canal and the Giudecca, the Baroque Church of Santa Maria della Salute (ABOVE) was built between 1631 and 1687, from plans drawn up by Baldassare Longhena. The plague had broken out in 1630, and the erection of the church fulfilled a vow made in an appeal for divine intervention to end the epidemic.

RIGHT: Here, Venice is traversed by the Grand Canal, its "artery of water," the Piazza San Marco, and the white-marble Church of Santa Maria della Salute. On 9 October 1786, Goethe exclaimed from the top of the campanile: "I see appearing all about terra firma where formerly there existed only the mirror of the waters." In the following century, Hippolyte Taine wrote: "…at night, in Venice, the churches and palaces transform themselves into giants and sail across the sea with the demeanor of ghosts."

George Sand declared in 1834: "No one prepared us for the beauty of the sky and the delight of Venice. The lagoon is so calm in the beautiful evenings that even the stars cease to quiver above. When one is at the center, [Venice] is so blue, so unified that the eye does not detect the horizon line, while the water and the sky dissolve into a continuous veil of azure, in which reverie loses its way and falls asleep....and from the top of Saint Mark's an immense sheet of bronze floats above my head."

The islands of the Venetian lagoon. On his return from the Holy Land in 1220, Saint Francis would have landed on San Francesco del Deserto, an islet that is today host to a Franciscan monastery (RIGHT). Torcello (BELOW) was once a flourishing town and the seat of a bishopric. Overtaken by the power of Venice and the curse of malaria, Torcello went into decline, beginning in the 11th century. An inscription in the baptistry states that the cathedral was erected in 639 on the orders of the military governor of the Byzantine Veneto to commemorate the courageous defense made against the invading Longobards. The 13th-century mosaic in the apse is a masterpiece of its kind.

On the islet of Burano, just above the level of the lagoon 9 kilometers from Venice, fishermen have adopted a varied palette to individualize their houses. Blues, greens, and a luminous array of ochres and pinks make a cheerful greeting for the constant stream of tourists arriving from all over the world to visit Burano's three famous churches: Santa Maria, San Fosco, and San Martino. The last contains a youthful work by Tiepolo. Burano is equally well known for its lace.

With its elliptical plan, vast size, and slender arcades, the arena at Verona, now some nineteen centuries old, speaks of the Roman origins and past of the city on the banks of the River Adige. Today the great theater is used to stage grand opera. Verona can justly claim to be, after Rome, the Italian city most endowed with Roman antiquities.

Padua in the Veneto.
With the common
purpose of
commemorating
Saint Anthony, the
Portuguese Franciscan
who died in Padua in
1231, artists of
different periods
lavished their talents on
the basilica dedicated
to the Saint, using four
different styles:
Romanesque,
Byzantine, Gothic, and
Perigordine. The
Basilica of Sant'Antonio
houses the tomb of the
eloquent preacher,
who evangelized
Africa and even
delivered a sermon to
the fishes. The great
church also contains art
works signed by such
masters as Donatello,
Altichieri, Bellano...

The Po delta in the Veneto. The longest river in Italy completes its course in five stages: the Po di Maestra, the Po della Pila, the Po della Gnocca, the Po di Tolle, and the Po di Goro, which form the delta. Here, after a run of 652 kilometers, the river flows quietly into the Adriatic.

The Venetian lagoon. For centuries, the coves and barriers of the Venetian lagoon have witnessed the tenacious energies of human beings, constantly vying with the waters for precious acres of land. However, the lagoon remains ever subject to the tides. Here, farming can only take place along the margins, and the villages look as if they had come straight from the realm of Lilliput.

In the polychrome geometry of the delta, where the Po flows at an average rate of 1,460 cubic meters per second, the signs of numerous interventions appear at regular intervals, all carved out by the government's hydraulic engineers for the purpose of taming the river's waters as they enter the Adriatic. Seen from the air, the technical skills required to achieve this control happens also to translate into a graphic expression worthy of the masters of radically abstract art.

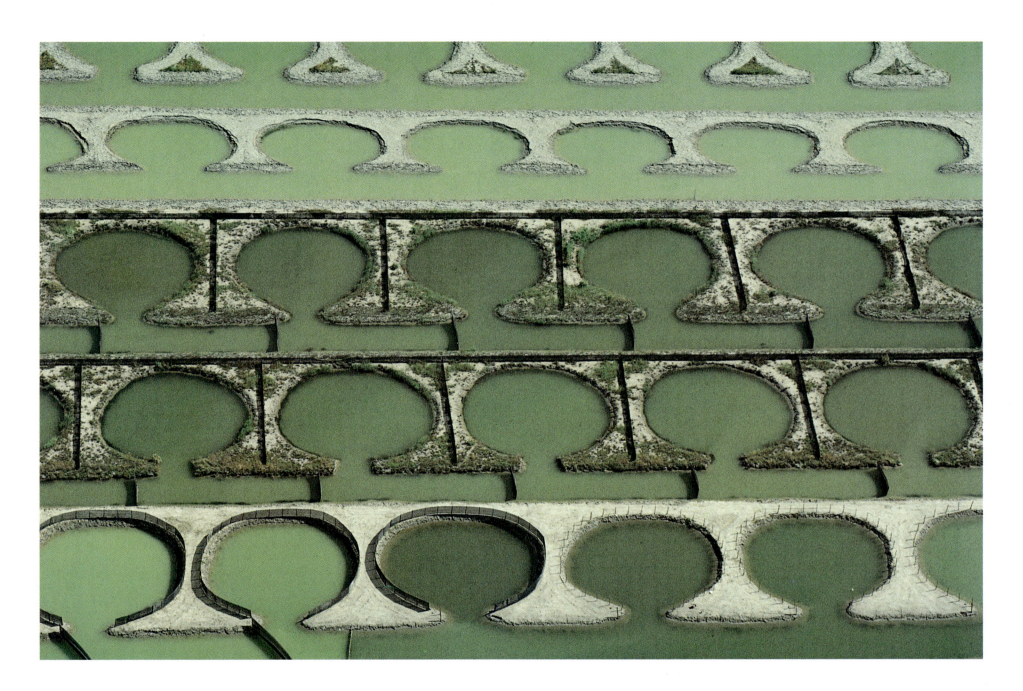

Despite the astonishing man-made geometry of these water-storage basins, the Po delta remains a desolate place and entirely dependent on the flooding of the river. But reclamation projects gradually yield positive results for the cultivation of rice and wheat.

The Apennine countryside. Scattered here and there throughout Emilia-Romagna are traces of the geological history of the region. A thousand years ago, the foothills of the Apennines were covered with trees. Today, forests grow on no more than 16 percent of the land. From above, the landscape, with its streams, crevasses, and valleys furrowed into clay hills by surface waters, takes on the appearance of a theater backdrop. The heights dominate the vast Emilian plain, formed in the Lower Paleolithic.

Thanks to new mechanical equipment, the farmers of Northern Italy have rationalized their agricultural production during the last several decades. As a result, they operate on an equal footing with their counterparts elsewhere in the European Community.

Piedmont gives priority to industrial development, which, for more than a century, has allowed the region to compete with the Germans, the French, and the Dutch. However, the province has not forgotten the traditions that bind its people to the soil. Italy's largest producer of rice, harvested in the Vercelli and Novara regions, Piedmont also holds its own in viticulture, the wines of the Asti and Cuneo districts being notable.

Genoa in Liguria.
"From a distance of six
or seven leagues, one
can already see her,
spread out in the recess
of her bay with the
nonchalant majesty of a
queen," wrote
Alexandre Dumas in
1841. Etymologically
derived from the Indo-
European *genu*, the
name Genoa
characterizes the gulf
as a mouth, very likely
meaning a well-
protected landing
place. At the end of the
3rd century, the
wardens of the port
and its pier became the
pioneers of an
institution that, over the
centuries, would make
the fortune of the
Genoese. This was the
alliance between those
responsible for
organizing the life of
the port and those who
managed the
institutions of the city.

Alassio, a town at the western end of the Ligurian Riviera, makes elegant use of its natural endowments. An exclusive seaside resort, Alassio is also famous for its 11th-century church, Sant'Amborgio, the Capuchin convent, and a pair of 17th-century oratories, one dedicated to Saint Catherine and the other to Saint Erasmus.

The symmetrical arrangement of the beach facilities on Alassio's seafront serves to enhance the effect of massed multicolored umbrellas. The town's name comes from *Alaxe*, which probably relates to the female name Adalaxia, itself a modified form of the Longobard Adalahis.

Portofino on the Riviera di Levante (the coast east of Genoa) in Liguria. Portus Delphini was the name Pliny the Elder gave to this cove, whose profile, when seen from the adjacent hill, resembles that of a dolphin. Once an overview reveals its sinuous shape cradled in a tree-covered hillside, Portofino can truly be said to possess the slenderness and grace of a marine mammal that hereabouts takes the place of a patron saint. The Riviera di Levante's "precious object of desire," Portofino offers many delights, but none greater than the harmony of the whole—pink or ochre houses, slate roofs, green shutters, the 15th-century fortress of San Giorgio, promontories almost tottering under their heavy vegetation, hills covered with olive trees, and the sea, unequaled in its emerald-green beauty.

From time immemorial, the tiny port of Camogli has been the traditional fishing preserve of sailors on Italy's Riviera di Levante. These masters of the sea can handle every kind of vessel, from yachts to large ocean-going liners. Camogli boasts two artistic jewels that form an integral part of its history—the Castel Dragonara and Luca Cambiaso's *Deposition* in the parish church of the Madonna dell'Assunzione.

In Camogli's dainty coves, tall houses and quays hug the shoreline. Documents dating from as early as the 12th century mention the serenity offered by this little Ligurian port, the last settlement on the southeastern arm of Genoa's bay.

THE HEART OF ITALY

Central Italy and its inhabitants embody a mixture of Northern rationality and an impulsive enthusiasm native to the Mezzogiorno or South. Their ultimate unity derives from a fusion of history as well as a mingling of peoples. Spread over almost 70,000 square kilometers, the region is notable for its sensitivity to the environment and its aptitude—its passion even—for the pleasures and labors of everyday life. It is flanked by two radically different seas—the marbled Tyrrhenian off the coast of Lazio and Tuscany on the west, and, to the east, the beloved Adriatic, which bathes not only the Romagnol Riviera but also the coast of the Marche and the Abruzzi. Only Umbria lacks access to the sea, which could make it appear to be Central Italy's most underendowed province. But Umbria will have none of this and indeed boasts of her riches—numerous works of art and a superb natural setting. After this brief introduction to the different regions at the heart of Italy, we can now discover their history, popular traditions, and enduring characteristics.

Quintina Sella, writing in 1876, said of Rome: "I should view it as a major disaster in the event Rome gained a large working class, because Rome, it seems to me, is where numerous issues requiring theoretical discussion and summoning all the intellectual forces of the nation ought to be debated. For this, however, the temperament of the great masses could prove troublesome. A body of that sort would be dangerous, or at least inappropriate, in my opinion." Actually, Rome is a neutral, tranquil capital, protected by geography from regional quarrels and responsible for maintaining equilibrium within a restless nation. Given this, one can distinguish Central Italy still more clearly, by focusing on its essential role, which is to stand for the country's balance of powers. The Latins, an autonomous people who were the first occupants of the territory known as Latium (modern Lazio), were already conscious of the political role the region would play. The presence in neighboring areas of Sabines, Samnites, Aequi, Hernici, Volsci, and, most of all, the Etruscans gave the whole territory a great density of populations. The cities of Latium joined together in a federation, a strongly religious league dominated by Alba Longa. Thanks, however, to a destiny reinforced by history, Rome emerged in the 7th century B.C., a city whose sociopolitical position the Middle Ages and subsequent eras would merely strengthen, granting her an overriding power never denied in the course of troubled centuries. The Vatican State, the eternal partner and all-important co-landlord, viewed the communes of Latium first as allies and then as enemies, just as it subsequently did the feudal castes during the inevitable confrontations with the masters of the Holy Roman Empire.

As of 1870, however, Lazio began to assume the geopolitical traits of an actual region. In that year, the last territories comprising the Papal States found themselves integrated into the colossal project of the Kingdom of Italy under the banner of Rome, the dominant province. The region around Latina

BELOW: Uccellina Park in Tuscany. At the entrance one finds this peremptory advice: "Respect nature in Uccellina Park; she will be grateful to you." PRECEDING PAGES: San Gimignano in Tuscany. Conceived as donjons or keeps, the 72 towers of *San Gimignano delle belle torri* were erected during the Middle Ages at the time of the struggles between the Guelphs and the Ghibellines. For reasons of prestige, the noble families involved in these costly disputes kept building their towers ever higher, always trying to outdo the enemy. Even today, San Gimignano bristles with fourteen towers, encircling ramparts, the 13th-century Palazzo del Podestà, and the Palazzao del Popolo dating from the 13th-14th centuries. In addition, the town has a fine cathedral, as well as double-tondo *Annunciation* by Filippino Lippi.

There are estimated to
be 97 major churches
and basilicas in the
Rome. Given this, it
would scarcely seem
fair to choose a few
random examples.
And so, during his
flight over the capital,
the photographer
settled for a pleasing
image of a church and
its dome seen against
trees shading the
adjacent cloister.

The little medieval town of Narni originated in Roman times and still sits proudly on the crest of a hill overlooking the olive groves in the valley of the River Nera.

benefited from a gigantic operation designed to drain the mosquito-infested marshes. This had been first attempted in the 2nd century B.C., followed by similar enterprises launched by Julius Caesar, several later Emperors, and then the Papacy during the 18th century. The results always fell short of expectations, and malaria continued to rage. In the 20th century, technological advance simplified the task, finally solving the problem forever. Today, the town of Latina ranks second only to Rome in urban population, a testimony, along with the area's architectural heritage, to political power at its most resolute.

Five provinces and 375 communes—this whole ensemble falls under the knowing influence of a city forced throughout the years to assume, in various forms, the difficult role of political mediator. The clear tendency to organize cities, such as Rieti, Viterbo, and Frosinone, had its origins in traditional prerogatives, as historical evidence affirms. Solid sociocultural roots have always had a direct impact on the potential to generate urban centers, both small and large. Quite apart from aesthetics, the triumph of Villanovan and then Etruscan cultures, the one Northern and the other Latin, as is typical of this southern locale, would not appear to be fortuitous. Tarquinia, a city in the province of Viterbo, would always be rich because of its ancient necropolis, whose thousands of funerary chambers decorated with paintings permit us to reconstruct the life and religion of the Etruscans. Rieti, at the geographical center of Italy, and the whole of Sabina are even more strikingly distinctive for their compelling fusion of history and nature.

Luxuriant, harmonious Tuscany was the region most favored by 19th-century travelers. Théophile Gautier, in his *Voyage en Italie*, shared his impressions: "At this point, one leaves Romagna to enter Tuscany, where one discovers an azure panorama of plains, mountains, and villages; a horizon dotted with cities and villas, shimmering in light and shade. When the slopes of the Apennines begin to descend towards Florence, sites increase in beauty. One senses the approach of a large, living city, a rare thing in Italy, that ossuary of dead towns." Tuscany divides into three parts. The first, which should be called Apennine, links Tuscany to Emilia and, above all, Bologna; the second owes its singularity to the fantastic forms of the hills of Chianti and the Val d'Elsa; and the third is dominated by the natural wonders of the Tyrrhenian coast with its fringe of hospitable islands. The major cities or towns—Florence, Pisa, Pistoia, Siena, Arezzo, Lucca, Grosseto, Leghorn, Massa Carrara—are the jewels of a territory rich in both natural and cultural assets. Fernand Braudel spoke of the Tuscan landscape as "the most moving in the world." A 20th-century historian with an international reputation, Braudel could legitimately evince the same thrill as an Impressionist painter. And little wonder, since Tuscany resembles the very ideal of an art museum, thanks to the canonic masters of art represented there, among them Leonardo da

These fields reflect the labor, perseverance, and good sense of the farmers who, generation after generation, created them. In Central and Southern Italy, crop rotation has become a regular practice, especially on small farms, the better to obtain a measure of stability in yield.

Constructed in the 16th century by the Spanish, the castle is not the only masterpiece to be found in L'Aquila, the provincial capital of the Abruzzi. A number of L'Aquila's churches are also important monuments, particularly the Basilica of Santa Maria di Collemaggio and the Basilica of San Bernardino, the latter a Renaissance building that houses the tomb of Saint Bernard of Siena.

Vinci and Michelangelo, of literature, such as Dante and the Bolognese Guido Cavalcanti, the Tuscan precursor of the *dolce stil nuovo* school of poetry, and finally of the political sciences at their apogee, in the person of Machiavelli, the author of *The Prince*. Tuscany never contested the position of agriculture in the regional economy. Once flourishing, farming and fishing retain an honorable place, but their status is more and more harnessed to the bumpy course of national and communal politics. On the other hand, the opportunities available to the tourist industry have always been immense—seas and mountains as well as cities full of art assure the region a steady flow of visitors responsive to the charms of the Tuscans.

The pre-Apennine plateau, which on the west extends across Umbria, imposes certain geographical restraints on the region. A large presence in the history of the peninsula, Umbria signifies traditional values within the panoply of qualities attributed to each of Italy's provinces. Modern-day Romans take great pleasure in the Umbrian countryside, which they can reach by automobile within an hour. A short while ago Todi, not far from Perugia, was voted "the world's most agreeable city to live in." Umbria incorporates 8,456 square kilometers, or 2.8 percent of Italian soil. On the map, the oval shape of the region inspires a certain sympathy, boxed in as it is by Lazio, Tuscany, and the Marche, their inviolable frontiers protecting the "green lungs" of Central Italy. Umbria takes pride in her arts, poets, and, most of all, her well-earned reputation for an all-enveloping mysticism. As the German art historian Carl Friedrich von Rumohr affirmed: "In the mid-15th century, or perhaps even earlier, the Umbrian schools of painting exercised a mystical appeal to which, in my opinion, every heart still opens because of a depth and delicacy of feeling, of a marvelous union of clear echoes from Early Christian art with the representations of the moderns. In reality, we should seriously consider the situation of the towns surrounding the Assisi hill, a place dedicated to Saint Francis. Standing close to the site where his order was founded, they must be prone to ideas and sentiments full of sweetness that no doubt helped raise modern painting to its zenith." It required the synthesizing capacity of von Rumohr to recognize those factors that created the myth of Umbria: Saint Francis, Perugino, a quiet simplicity of feeling, and the quality of the environment.

An almost perfect rectangle—an atypical shape in Italy's topography—identifies the Marche, a region just slightly larger than neighboring Umbria but richer in natural wonders. Extremely mountainous at the center, where the summit of Mount Vettore in the Sybilline chain is 2,476 meters above sea level, the Marche drop down to the Adriatic coast. Together, such characteristics are more or less common to Emilia-Romagna and the Abruzzi as well; still, they leave the Marche afflicted with a slight inferiority complex vis-à-vis Tuscany and Umbria. At the same time, the Marche have had an enthralling history. And what attention the region has devoted to training people, through schooling and apprenticeships, for trade and industry! As in Tuscany, there are three different aspects to the Marche. Traditionally rural, the first part was until recently parceled out among more than 100,000 farms, places much cherished by the public. The second part comprises a number of cities, such as Pesaro, Fano, and Ancona, which form a string of beacons along the seashore, a sandy, flat terrain everywhere except between San Bartolo and the Conero massif overlooking the Adriatic. Finally, the Marche have a mountainous aspect, which makes it difficult to imagine how this central section of Italy, with its high, rugged environment, could nonetheless harbor towns and abbeys like Camerino, Fabriano, Novafeltria, and San Leo. The very consonance of the word "mark"—which means boundary marker, the etymological root of Marche—takes us back to the Carolingian and then the Germanic empires. The name, with its seemingly built-in fate, has in no way prevented the region from generating vigorous sociocultural movements. Of its four universities, those at Urbino, Macerata, and Camerino are very old. The one at Ancona, a modern addition to the area's academic ensemble, benefits a growing body of students from other provinces. At Recanati we discover the world evoked by Giacomo Leopardi, but the "Infinity" hill and the little piazza of "Saturday in the Village" no longer deserve the adjectives that the great poet applied to his home town, which he called "vile and vulgar."

An aerial view of the Abruzzi reveals a land whose cultural makeup is lyrical but whose physical structure is full of harsh contrasts. The region's traditional name clearly suggests a territory divided into a multitude of different zones forever in the throes of overcoming troublesome obstacles in order to achieve geographical and socioeconomic integration. The Abruzzi have always been attuned to Neapolitan culture. At the same time, massive emigration exposed the ills that long plagued the region. In the wake of the flight to Rome at the end of the 19th century, then to the North, and next across the ocean, a recent statistic is enough to give an idea of the magnitude of the outflow. Between 1960 and 1970, more than 200,000 Abruzzese abandoned their lands to search for a different reality. The phenomenon can be easily explained, since agriculture is synonymous with meager yields. Sheep-rearing suffered from the cost of labor, and, despite the length of the coast, fishing can no longer to considered the main driving force of the regional economy. Still, the natural, cultural, and artistic ramparts of the Abruzzi stand in valiant defense of the province's image. Primarily, these consist of the Roman heritage—the theaters at Amiternum, Pietrabbondante, and Teramo, as well as the archaeological zones of Alba Fucentia and Sepino. Equally important perhaps is Pescara, the birthplace of Gabriele D'Annunzio, poet and warrior, whom many viewed as the greatest of all the Abruzzese ramparts.

The Maiella range in the Abruzzi. From its summit— Mount Morrone, with an altitude of 2,795 meters—the Maiella offers climbers a view over the Tyrrhenian and Adriatic seas. Visitors who linger there overnight will enjoy an unforgettable explosion of color at dawn.

Nestled among the twists, turns, and spines of Tuscany's Apuan Alps are the Carrara marble quarries from which Michelangelo obtained material for his sculptures. Centuries before, the Romans, who spoke of *lunensi* marbles (for Luni, a nearby town), had a tradition of facing their sumptuous villas with this prized white, crystalline limestone. The color range of the material is incomparable, for, in addition to the dazzling white of the "statuary" marble, the *badiglio* variety runs a subtle gamut from gray-black to bluish, passing through violet, peach blossom, and floral tones.

The quarries of the Apuan Alps yield stone of such whiteness that their appearance is sometimes mistaken for permanent snow cover. The marble is cut into blocks and dispatched to the coastal plain for further processing. When exported, the cut stone leaves from the nearby port of Marina di Carrara.

The Republic of San Marino, a sovereign enclave within Italy south of Rimini, is one of the world's smallest states and the oldest republic in Europe. Its independence dates from 855. Medieval in appearance, the town occupies a formidable rocky spur. A tower and a pair of *rocche* or fortresses crown the three punctuating outcrops, while a high battlemented wall completely encircles the clustered town, from which the view extends as far as the coast of Dalmatia.

The Republic of San Marino has its own currency, maintains its own army and police force, issues stamps, and, every six months, elects a new pair of Captain-Regents, from members of the Grand Council, to head the government. At the beginning of the 19th century, the Republic indulged itself in the luxury of rejecting Napoleon's proposals for expansion. A neutral state, San Marino provided safe haven for Garibaldi in 1849 and for numerous refugees during the Second World War.

Loreto in the Marche. The sanctuary of the *Santa Casa*, a structure dating from the Gothic and Renaissance periods, owes much to the contributions made by important architects such as Maiano, Sangallo for the dome, Bramante for the side chapels, and Vanvitelli for the 18th-century campanile. According to legend, *la Santa Casa*—the House of Mary—was miraculously transported here from Nazareth in 1291 by angels who supposedly deposited the relic in a laurel wood (*lauretum* in Latin, hence Loreto).

The Middle Ages and the Renaissance presided over the growth of the legendary town of Loreto. And "legendary" is the proper word, considering the intensely mystical atmosphere that has always been felt here.

Day after day, devout pilgrims file into the sanctuary, with the conviction that they are praying before the house of the Blessed Virgin, a small Romanesque building for which Donato Bramante designed a marble screen.

Left: The jealous care with which Urbino preserves its buildings and architectural wonders inherited from the past does not prevent the town from living in the present with enviable vigor. The university, among the most lively in the Marche, and the brilliant Academy of Fine Arts enjoy immense prestige in the community. In former times, Duke Federigo da Montefeltro, a great patron of the humanities, had become known as the "Light of Italy."

Above: A view over part of the town, showing its lanes, palaces, small courtyards, bell towers and Roman tiles, ramparts and pale-rose brickwork.

Castelfidardo in the Marche played its most dramatic role on the stage of history during the 1860s, when it became the scene of a thunderous battle between the Piedmontese and the forces of the Papal States. Thanks to the victory won by the former, the Marche became part of the Kingdom of Italy. A depiction of the military engagement can be found in a watercolor by Francesco Hayez, now in the collection of the Castello Sforzesco in Milan.

A quasi-religious passion for the accordion has won a worldwide reputation for this small town. Castelfidardo is to the making of accordions just as Cremona is to the fabrication of violins. Born in 1822 of the little harmonica, the accordion has since had a museum dedicated to it in Castelfidardo.

The walled town of Gubbio occupies the slopes of Mount Ingino. The ochre of the stones and the "burnt bread" of the roofs, the absence of trees, the hermitages clinging to the steep cliffs, the austerity of the buildings—all combine to give Gubbio a sober, grave appearance. Every year on 15 May, a festival unfolds in the historic center, among the shops selling ceramics, patrician houses, and the Ducal as well as Council palaces. Dressed in traditional costumes, artisans, students, and farmers join in a frenzied race, bearing on their shoulders statues of Saints Ubaldo, Anthony, and George hoisted on the tips of *ceri*, wooden "candles" 4 meters long. The festival commemorates Gubbio's miraculous victory in 1151 over a formidable coalition of eleven rival towns.

The peaceful façade of the Basilica of Saint Francis and its monastery at Assisi. This church may have been the most richly invested with artistic treasures during the Middle Ages. In 1228, Pope Gregory IX, author of the *Decretals*, laid the first stone for the basilica, which would also house the tomb of the Saint. In an abrupt departure from Byzantine concepts, the architectural mass encourages meditation, while the spring of the high ogival vaults inspires prayer. A new realist art reflecting the Franciscan spirit, especially the principle of simplicity, came into being at Assisi. The exquisite frescoes by Giotto and his assistants narrate the life of Christ and the miracles of Saint Francis.

From the time of the Romans, the enviable strategic position of Assisi virtually dictated that the place become a *municipium*. Then came the crisis of the Imperial era, which opened the way for the barbarian invasions, while also proving to be a extremely fertile period in both artistic and religious terms. The presence and acts of Saint Francis brought this little town of 25,000 souls international fame quite disproportionate to its actual size.

Here the way in which the medieval town was conceived can be seen to perfection. The French historian Ernest Renan, who at the end of the 19th century "took such pains" to reach Assisi, was overwhelmed when he saw it and gave a loving account of his experience. The artists who contributed to the beauty and spiritual grandeur of Assisi were primarily Giotto, Cimabue, Simone Martini, and both Piero and Ambrogio Lorenzetti.

Città di Castello in Umbria. Art has always reigned supreme in this little town, known in Roman times as Tifernum. The early inhabitants did much to strengthen the cultural ties between the Romans and the Umbrians. Beginning in the 16th century, an elegant court life developed here, thanks to the Vitelli family, feudal lords of Città di Castello. Raphael, Andrea and Domenico della Robbia, and Vasari all placed their genius in the service of this pretty town on the left bank of the Tiber.

The Duomo or Cathedral of Spoleto, built in the 12th century near the top of the hill on which the town stands, presides over a well-ordered piazza paved in rose-colored brick. The severe façade is fronted by a charming Renaissance loggia added in the 15th century. Every summer the population of Spoleto becomes involved in the Festival of the Two Worlds, an elegant cultural event founded in 1958 and dedicated to music and theater, staged mostly in the Piazza del Duomo.

Only reluctantly does anyone take leave of Spoleto, crowned by the Rocca (castle of the Popes). Here, harmony of the sweetest sort reigns between the lime trees and the pink-paved Piazza del Duomo, the Roman aqueduct and the fountains, the evergreen oaks and the Arch of Drusus, the festival's fanfares, the silent tomb of Fra Filippo Lippi, and the enormous "stabile" or steel sculpture by Alexander Calder in the Station Square. The general view (right) reveals, in all its glory, a town that has successfully integrated the present with a love of tradition. In the background, on the left, can be seen the buff-pink façade of the cathedral and its slender bell tower.

A volcanic outcrop provided the site for the town of Orvieto, with its cathedral and palaces. The cathedral's façade is often deemed the boldest and richest in all of Italian Gothic. It is estimated that some 33 architects, 152 sculptors, 68 painters, and 90 mosaicists figured among the artists who, during the 13th and 14th centuries, contributed to the achievement of this masterpiece. Although originally Etruscan, Orvieto is indebted to the Longobards for the rudiments of its urban culture. Then, shortly after the year 1000, the signs of a local aesthetic began to emerge. The sheer diversity of the architecture in Orvieto is remarkable. Several monuments were constructed using local volcanic rock, and the numerous towers include the square *del Moro* tower, the 16th-century clock tower, the twelve-sided Romanesque tower, and the medieval towers of the old quarter.

A village in Umbria. The rooftops celebrate the Roman tile—light, effective, gently rounded, and cheap. It can be seen here from every angle. Architects and roofers probably miss the time when the irregularities of hand-wrought tiles made it possible to give the shape or design of a roof an appearance unlike any other.

Space and time deserve equal credit for the exemplary appearance of this little Umbrian town. The vertical sides of the medieval keep and the long horizontal forms of the structures flanking it lend stability to the gentle curves of streets and houses that faithfully follow the rising terrain.

Surrounding the Piazza della Republica in Foligno are the cathedral, the Palazzo Communale (town hall), and the Palazzo Trinci, a curious hybrid composed of a 15th-century building and a 19th-century façade. In the course of a long history, this town on the plain has often been involved with leading figures such as Liutprand, King of the Lombards (713–744), Frederick I Barbarossa (1152–90), the Guelfs and the Ghibellines (1076–1250). Today, Foligno is a center for commercial activity.

The Duomo or Cathedral of Siena features striking contrasts in its polychrome or black-and-white striped marbles. A welcoming inscription above the Camollia gate reads: *Cor magis tibi Sena pandit* ("Siena opens its heart wide to you"). The central feature of this universally loved city is without question the rose-colored Piazza del Campo, with its "fountain of joy" dating from the 15th century.

The old city of Lucca, with its ancient ramparts and bastions, is encircled by a splendid promenade, 4 kilometers in length and shaded by plane trees, limes, and venerable elms. The colors of Lucca are the red of brick and the green of the public parks. Only in an aerial view does the city reveal the riches of its private gardens, hidden by high walls from passers-by. Pragmatic and cultivated, the Lucchese have lived in peace since 1369, when they purchased their independence from the Pisans for the sum of 100,000 florins. The Roman plan of the city can still be seen, with its houses grouped about the oval site of the amphitheater.

FOLLOWING PAGES: The 16th-century Spanish fort of Porto Ercole dominates the Orbetello lagoon.

The Ponte Vecchio in Florence, the most famous bridge over the River Arno, was constructed in 1345 as a sober, functional structure. Two centuries later it was embellished with shops offering the wares of craftsmen, jewelers, and silversmiths, which still give the bridge its unique quality and irresistible appeal. Above the shops, Vasari added a covered corridor linking the Uffizi Galleries and the Palazzo Pitti.

The extraordinary triptych of monuments, built between the 13th century and the 15th, consists of the Duomo, or cathedral, the cost of which was met by the Florentine Republic with the help of the weavers' guild; the Baptistry, a structure as famous for its bronze doors as for its mosaics; and the Campanile, based on plans by Giotto, who, in 1334, initiated the construction work. The other masters involved in this unique ensemble were Arnolfo di Cambio, Andrea Pisano, and Brunelleschi, who designed the majestic cupola in polychrome marble that crowns the Duomo.

The Umbrian countryside. In these calm and untroubled surroundings, only the cypresses strike a vertical note. By some magical means, the somber, slender cypresses-elsewhere associated with cemeteries-become in Italy a symbol of pratician grace.

Chianti! The very name is a wonderful reminder of this gentle region. A full-bodied wine with a piquant flavor, Chianti originates from vineyards on the friendly hills of Tuscany, around the villages of Gaiole, Castellina, Radda, Greve. The region also produces olive oil of an exceptional quality.

The eastern Apennines. This old Benedictine monastery has retained its tranquil atmosphere, cradled at the center of well-ordered fields and plantations. The harmony of curves, the serenity of cypresses, and the purety of the sky can be found together almost everywhere in the Tuscan countryside, endlessly repeated until they become a leitmotif of the region.

ABOVE: Rome's Tiber Island, which, according to legend, came into being when the Romans dumped a vast amount of wheat in order to offend the Tarquins, who had been expelled from the city. The islet remains one of the capital's most romantic sites. Here one can still take a gentle stroll, a pleasure no longer available in neighboring Trastevere, where the automobile is sovereign king.

RIGHT: The Castel Sant'Angelo and the Basilica of Saint Peter. The delays that pilots encounter as they await permission to land at Rome Airport provide a certain compensation for anxious passengers, who are treated to a sensational view of the Eternal City from the air. As this photograph reveals, Rome is a city of striking contrasts, at once ancient and modern, nonchalant and frenetic.

Saint Peter's Square in Vatican City. The supreme honor of building this magnificent piazza fell to Gianlorenzo Bernini, the architect responsible for the majority of Rome's important Baroque structures. The monumental ensemble, which celebrates the triumph of Christianity, comprises 284 columns disposed along the arcs of two embracing arms. It symbolizes the ideal of perfection that the Papacy had always attempted to set before the world's faithful. Begun in 1656 and completed eleven years later, in 1667, Bernini's scheme incorporated the Egyptian obelisk installed by Sixtus V in 1586 and included more than 140 statues representing apostles, saints, and popes.

Rome's Piazza Navona is known to the entire world as the "children's square." During the Christmas season, the piazza all but disappears under the toys, gifts, and sweets destined exclusively for Roman children, too young to understand the distinguished history of the surroundings. The Piazza Navona preserves the elongated form of the Greek stadium that the Emperor Domitian offered to the populace in A.D. 86 as a place for games and races. Navona is derived from *agon*, the Greek word for "contest." In 1651, Bernini created the *Fountain of Four Rivers*, which stands before the striking façade of the Church of Sant'Agnese, designed by his rival, Francesco Borromini.

A well-preserved monument of ancient Rome, the amphitheater inaugurated in A.D. 80 at the behest of the Emperor Flavius Vespasianus. The colossal statue of Nero installed there caused the arena to become known as the Colosseum. With a circumference of 350 meters and a height of 48 meters, the Colosseum was then the world's largest building. It could accommodate up to 50,000 people at spectacles involving chariot races and various sorts of contest.

ABOVE: The Pantheon. Destroyed by fire, the Pantheon was rebuilt in A.D. 118 at the command of the Emperor Hadrian. The Barberini Pope, Urban VIII, allowed Bernini to strip away vast amounts of the Pantheon's bronze fittings as raw material for casting the *Apostle's Chair* in Saint Peter's. RIGHT: The Piazza del Popolo in Rome. Even today, this square is the true center of the Eternal City. However, a solemn atmosphere emerges from the architecture of the piazza's three religious buildings: the twin churches of Santa Maria in Montesanto and Santa Maria dei Miracoli and, sheltered by the Porta Flaminia, the Church of Santa Maria del Popolo. Renaissance in origin but altered during the Baroque era, Santa Maria del Popolo possesses two masterpieces by Caravaggio: *The Conversion of Saint Paul* and *The Crucifixion of Saint Peter*.

SOUTHERN ITALY

In 1928, Walter Benjamin noted that "it is easy to love Naples when one sees it from the sea." However, this idyllic view quickly evaporates under the critical eye of a German philosopher eager to penetrate a redoubtable city's most intimate and sometimes less than honorable secrets: "As soon as one sets foot on dry land . . . on a pavement eternally shaken by Vesuvius, or one seeks accommodation in chock-full hotels, things begin to take on a different aspect. . . ." Benjamin launches a two-pronged attack, one on the Neapolitans themselves and the other on Jakob Job, the author of a book about Naples, ". . . because Job says nothing of Piedigrotta, the noisy bacchanalia during the night of 8 September, or the gigantic feasts in which the Neapolitans participate by making a weekly payment of a few pennies to their butcher (the people of the North pay their life insurance by the same system) for the sake of indulging themselves in total gluttony when the moment comes." The diatribe continues, now taking aim at the petty thieves who prowl the train station or the din of shiny new motorcycles that roar through the city. But if modern Naples leaves Benjamin vexed and chronically irritated, those 18th-century Grand Tourists who kept diaries found the great city enchanting and never ceased to praise it, the mother of the entire bay. Benjamin may have been influenced by earlier French, German, and English travelers who, from 1500 to 1700, characterized their visits to Naples as a disheartening experience and the mythic sites as haunted by frightful ghosts. Schott took the Mondragone for the cave of a dragon that "kills and devours whoever comes near," while Bouchard affirms that, under the "cruel mountain," "seven powerful kings defend their treasure chests overflowing with pearls, amber, gold, and diamonds." Even the Italians take part in this chorus of gruesome memories. Celano visited the villa at Poggio Reale and noted that "the reputation of its celebrated fountains has vanished because of greedy and dishonest people who carried off the underground lead pipes." As for Bourguinon Président de Brosse, he passed the blame around instead of piling the whole of it on the local citizenry. Following his visit to the Royal Palace, he castigated "those barbarous Spaniards who, for three months, left the pictures from the Farnese Collection in a stairwell without light. Meanwhile, everyone went there to urinate. Yes sir, they urinated on Guido Reni and Correggio."

Naples seems destined to incite extreme and contradictory feelings. In 1530, Bernardino Fuscano evoked the majesty of the city, "her temples, her gilded loggias, her opulent architecture, her grand public buildings, her palaces, her statues, and her paintings." A century later, Hieronymus Welsch spoke of his delight over the troupes of tumblers and circus performers, the cascades of flowers and confetti,

PRECEDING PAGES: In the 1960s, the town of Tropea in Calabria was much admired for its simplicity, the beauty of its natural environment, and the friendliness of its people. A pioneer in the realm of holiday tourism, Tropea has paid a price for taking this lead. Now, with a kind of aloof elegance, the town has become resigned to playing the role of "historic glory." LEFT: Scilla dominates the Straits of Messina, situated as the town is between Bagnara Calabra to the north and Villa San Giovanni to the south, the point of embarkation for Sicily. The castle offers an ideal position from which to observe the efforts of the fishermen to catch swordfish.

The famous reefs at Capo Vaticano suggest the hand of some toppled colossus or a group of dozing crocodiles. More simply, one can also admire the beauty of this geological phenomenon and the clarity of the colors on the Calabrian coast.

the fireworks on the sea. Goethe declared that he preferred Naples to Rome, which he found to be an "old monastery." Alfred de Musset urged that one go see Naples at the earliest possible opportunity instead of just dreaming about it: "There is scarcely anyone who has never wanted to visit Naples. As for myself, I yearned for it so long that I ended up creating in my mind's eye a half-true, half-imaginary Naples that I have had to demolish altogether." On the other hand, Bouchard viewed things quite differently when he wrote that in Naples "there are a few handsome palaces and a hundred mean, squat little dwellings."

Even today, in the dizzying maze of its lanes and alleys, lower Naples remains very much as it was in the 17th century, to the joy of those with a taste for what they see as Neapolitan picturesque. Satisfactions of this sort—"the silent pleasure," as Goethe called it—are there to be had at every corner, and in this visitors will not be disappointed. Should they wish to seek out early Naples, as it was, for instance, in the Roman period, they will find the remains of a theater and the temple of the Dioscuri, as well as *terme* or baths. They can also extend their itinerary deep into the catacombs of Saint Januarius, a subterranean world embellished with frescoes and mosaics. The following centuries left an incomparable mix of artistic monuments representative of every epoch, from the Cathedral (1323) and the Church of Saint Clare (1328) to the Castel Nuovo, erected by Pierre d'Agincourt and modeled on the Château d'Angers, and the Castel Sant'Elmo. From this period dates the great altarpiece dedicated to Saint Louis of Toulouse, executed by Simone Martini for Robert of Anjou, and the works of Giotto that adorn the Castel Nuovo and the Church of Saint Clare.

After the Renaissance, represented by Francesco Laurana, Giuliano da Maiano, Nicolò dell'Arca, and Francesco di Giorgio Martini, come the masterworks of Caravaggio, Ribera, Domenichino, Aniello Falcone, Salvator Rosa, Giordano, and Solimena. For still-life painting there are the canvases of Ruoppolo, Forte, and Recco. Meanwhile, the architects Domenico Fontana, Ferdinando Fuga, Giovanni and Antonio Medrano, and Luigi Vanvitelli created respectively such remarkable buildings as the Royal Palace, the hospital for the poor, the royal palace and park of Capodimonte, the San Carlo Opera, the royal residence at Caserta, and the Church of the Trinity. Certainly, the city's museums deserve—indeed demand—and will reward several days of special attention: the Museo Nazionale, with its collection of Classical sculpture, the national galleries at Capodimonte, and the Villa Floridiana, which houses the ceramics collection of the Museo Principe Diego Aragona Pignatelli Cortes. These treasures blend with the fabulous patrimony of Campania, an area rich in ancient

Tropea merges with its rock foundations adjacent to white-sand beaches and a clear sea, which combine to make the town a very choice site.

history and unforgettable sites: Oscan Capua, which Livy recalled as the largest, wealthiest, and most famous of Italic cities, while citing Avellino and Cumae for their ceramics; the temples and tombs at Paestum; and the villas at Herculaneum and Pompeii, obliterated when Vesuvius erupted in A.D.79.

Finally, there is the Sorrentine peninsula—notable for its nature preserves, its fruits, its wines with their earthy tang, and its intense artistic development—which appeals most of all because of its seductive landscape and the mildness of its climate. Inland, one can still meditate within the last enclave of an archaic life, a world of tiny, almost invisible hamlets, perched on sheer cliffs or wooded heights, as if there to affirm a reassuring physical continuity with nature.

Basilicata, once almost inaccessible, offers guests a historic heritage unique in Italy for its cave dwellings known to the world as the *sassi di Matera*. For centuries, and probably since A.D. 400, Matera—which long served as the capital of Basilicata, a position held since 1806 by Potenza—drew multitudes of rural families who took up residence in grottoes cut into solid tuff, often accompanied by their draft animals, used to work the fields, and always escorted by Catholic priests, who built places of worship right in the same troglodite havens. Today, almost all the *sassi* are empty, leaving Matera with only a few potters in residence, along with its churches, some of which retain their primitive frescoes. The singularity of this Basilicatan town derives from its surprising resemblance to the cave settlements of Cappadocia in Turkey, several thousand kilometers from Matera.

At the beginning of the 19th century, few foreigners on their Grand Tour dared travel into Southern Italy as far as Apulia and Calabria, an enterprise that appeared as dangerous as the expeditions into the heart of Black Africa several decades later. Even Stendhal, no doubt fearful of the perilous journey, settled for inventing an account of a pseudo-visit to the far South in order to complete the second edition of his *Rome, Naples, and Florence*. Yet, from as early as the 16th century, some brave souls did venture into the region. For five years, from 1575 to 1580, the Dominican priest Serafino Razzi traveled through the countryside and the coastal areas populated two millennia earlier by the citizens of Magna Graecia. The world he describes is not tempting: "Countrysides without trees or villages, hills made more for pack animals and goats than for men." Then, a bit further along, he says of Capitanata (the province of Foggia): "A dreadfully unhealthy province; the air is not good, water scarce, and it is prostrated by terrible heat and heavily infested with snakes. The people are unfit for labor, the horses devoid of strength. Since there are no rivers, the wheat is ground by machines driven by men, horses,

Atrani, on the Amalfi coast, is a very old village within this coastal microcosm in the province of Salerno. Here, the two buildings of special interest are the Church of San Salvatore near the viaduct, founded in the 10th century, and the collegiate Church of Saint Mary Magdalene, which dates from 1274.

The plan of the Church of the Madonna del Buon Consiglio, in the Capodimonte quarter of Naples, is the same as that of Saint Peter's in Rome but on a smaller scale. All about stand the serried ranks of buildings erected since the Second World War. "During the years when the royalist shipping magnate Achille Lauro served as mayor, the city was left wide open to all manner of exploitation," according to the Neapolitan writer Raffaele La Capria. "Overbuilding went on to the point of indecency, fueled by the greed of Naples' construction industry."

and other pack animals. The inhabitants of Apulia suffer from the lack of potable water, and I have even seen cats drink from a holy-water basin." Curiously, the writings of Leandro Alberti, dated 1550, deliver a more positive message: "A happy country Calabria, its sites resemble a paradise on earth. . . . Here, wheat, barley, and wines of every quality abound; here wine and hemp came into the world; and manna falls from Heaven; the gardens are full of lemon and orange trees in all varieties." Whatever their faults or virtues of yore, Apulia and Calabria have now caught up with the march of time. Natural forces will always be powerful there, but the lands have been taken over by the emissaries of modern industry. Factories, refineries, marinas, and accommodations for tourists have invaded the coast and, in the form of so-called "villages," the ancient forests as well.

The San Paolo Stadium in Naples is dedicated to *calcio*, otherwise known as football. Here the *tifosi* give full rein to their passions.

Despite this, the past remains strongly imprinted upon both these regions, and mysterious, sometimes indecipherable messages, left by so many different peoples, speak to us of art and history. Two great archaeological finds have recently been made in Calabria and Apulia, one in 1972 and the other in 1976. The first involves a pair of monumental bronze statues, come upon accidentally by a diver some 300 meters offshore from the marina at Riace, and the second the treasure excavated from a necropolis near Rutigliano a few kilometers south of Bari. The two statues lost at sea and the ambers, ceramics, and bronzes discovered in sixty sarcophagi in the environs of Bari date from the same era, between the 6th and the 5th centuries B.C. The bronze giants, which measure about 2 meters high, take us back, most assuredly, to a time of great brilliance in Greek sculpture, and the possibility cannot be excluded that they originated in the school of Phidias. As for the objects and arms from the Rutigliano necropolis, they prove that, in addition to art works created on the eastern side of the Adriatic, the period produced still others on the Italian side—especially at Taranto—which found favor throughout Magna Graecia.

In 1970, in Apulia, an earlier and totally fortuitous discovery had brought to light the cave paintings of Porto Badisco near Otranto. There are hundreds of them, all red or brown, probably executed some 6,000 years ago by men who assembled in this grotto and made it their sanctuary.

Throughout the region the artistic genius of the people gave rise to an architecture with an incomparable aesthetic, evident in the 13th-century Castel del Monte, which reflects the architectural ideals of Frederick II, as well as in the great castles at Gioia del Colle and Lucera, these too either built or enlarged by Frederick. The Gothic and Renaissance styles of Meridional Italy have often been noted; however, it is the Baroque that had the most striking influence upon the area's

The Alberobello *trulli*. Exclusive to Apulia, these small, seemingly uniform habitations occasionally sport emblems that distinguish one house from the other: crosses, statues, or symbols whose meaning remains obscure. As enigmatic as Sardinia's *nuraghi,* the *trulli* have their origins in prehistoric civilizations.

urbanism and building. This is particularly true at Lecce, whose Baroque typifies the period, even if the real masterpieces came into full bloom at Martina Franca, Bitonto, Barletta, Bari, and Trani. In 1890 an amazed Paul Bourget wrote: "If the legendary boot that forms Italy bore a spur, the dear city of Lecce occupies the exact place of the rowel. It is such an enchanting, precious jewel of a city, and I immediately succumbed to a great warmth of feeling for the place. Before coming here, I attached to the terms Baroque and Rococo only a sense of the disagreeable and the pretentious. Lecce would have taught me that they can also be synonymous with light fantasy, giddy elegance, and happy grace. The entire city is nothing, so to speak, but sculpture and delicacy."

The history of Calabria—from the Greeks to the Lucanians and the Romans, from the Longobards to the Byzantines, from the Saracens to the Normans, from the Swabians to the Anvegins, from the Aragonese to the Bourbons and the French—is an uninterrupted sequence of foreign occupations, of guerrilla resistance, and the inevitable repressions throughout some three millennia. And all those who attempted to dominate the region sought to record their presence on its coasts and mountains in some indelible way. The earliest periods bear the names of the legendary and immensely wealthy Sipari, of Crotone and Reggio, colonized by the Greeks around the 8th century B.C., of Locri and Caulonia. Then, over the course of time, came the grand medieval, Byzantine, and Romanesque phases, just as in neighboring Apulia. The churches of Basilicata at Stilo la Cattolica and San Giovanni Vecchio date from the Middle Ages, while the ensemble of Byzantine and Romanesque churches, especially the little 12th-century Church of the Panaglia, are characteristic of Rossano, which was the most Byzantine city in Calabria. As for Norman influences, they can be seen at their most powerful in the cathedrals of Tropea and Gerace, as well as in the castle at Cosenza, where the Romanesque and the Gothic all but fuse in the cathedral. These high medieval styles can also be found in the cathedral at Santa Severina. Meanwhile, the Baroque positively abounds, in the collegiate Church of the Magdalene at Morano, in the sanctuary at Paola, and in the churches of Sant'Anna and Santa Caterina at Gerace. The countless gold or silver objects, scattered more or less everywhere as a means of propagating the faith among the masses, are often the work of Calabrese artists as talented as they are anonymous.

"The nation is greater than your father or your mother," declared Socrates to Crito, "and, whatever the violence or the injustice she may do to us, we must obey her without flinching." Thus did the Greeks and Romans understand life. Mix in the imaginative, extraverted temperament of Southern Italians, and it becomes clear how such a conception of *civitas* could invest their souls with a deep, emotional source of loyalty to their city.

The first convulsions of Vesuvius gave rise to many apocalyptic legends. Very likely the oldest of the volcano's cones, called Mount Somma, was formed during the Quaternary era. Although two other equally powerful eruptions have completely altered the surrounding area, heedless people continue to build their houses on the mountain's lower slopes.

Baroque buildings and motifs abound in the historic center of Lecce. This town—an ancient Roman *municipium*, Lupiae—is today known as "the Baroque Florence." From the 16th century to the 18th, local architects and sculptors vied with one another in their inventive creations, aided by the soft, golden limestone of the region, a fine-grained material that is highly suited to cutting and carving. Lecce's urban fabric is especially impressive, including a wealth of palaces, piazzas, monasteries, churches, and chapels.

Like some brilliant white temple, the town of Ostuni, in Apulia, overlooks the sea a short distance away. In the background of the photograph seen here, the beach area is dotted with statuesque, centuries-old trees. The 16th-century cathedral has a curious, countercurving outline.

The Greek colonists who landed on the coast of Apulia no doubt recognized the aesthetic qualities of this site, since they dubbed their settlement Gallipoli, "beautiful city." With its ramparts rising directly out of the water, the castle of Frederick II watches over the old port.

Gallipoli is one of the most beautiful ports in Apulia. The old town, situated on a small island, is reached from the new town by a bridge.

Preceding pages:
Curious buildings
fashioned of dry stone,
the domed *chiancarelle*,
which abound in the
region, and the
Alberobello *trulli* (p.
146) look as if they
might feature in a fairy
tale. The Mediterranean
people were not
individualists; on the
contrary, they preferred
a communal, unified
existence. Alberobello
and similar towns are
called "villages of lime,"
since both the interiors
of the *trulli*, where each
room is roofed with a
dome of the exact size,
and their exterior walls
are frequently renewed
with whitewash.

OPPOSITE AN RIGHT: Vast clay-like fields and unstable rocky outcrops from the desolate landscape of Basilicata, seventy percent of whose population still work the soil. However, yields here are poor, and increasingly young people leave the area to seek more rewarding employment in the industries of the North.

Throughout the centuries, people have sought to provide themselves with protection by building on rocky features in the landscape, as seen here in Matera, a town in Basilicata. The history of the place is easily detected from the top of the 13th-century campanile. From this vantage point, one can survey the unfinished Tramontano castle, the streets, the palaces, and churches in Gothic or Baroque styles. However, from the panoramic route along the wild gorge, where the lower part of the town is all but deserted, one may yet hear the murmur of people bound to live in narrow caves, the *sassi*, in company with their draft animals. The modern town, a lively center, occupies the higher ground.

Another market town
in Matera province,
where erosion has cut
deep gorges, leaving
Basilicata a desolate
region of vast
horizons. The villages,
generally built on high
ground above ravines,
consist of little
whitewashed houses
huddled together so
tightly they can
scarcely be
distinguished from
one another.

LEFT: A general view of Naples, the provincial capital of Campania. Almost everyone taking the Grand Tour in the 18th and 19th centuries succumbed to the charms of Naples. On 8 March 1817, Stendhal noted in his journal: "I depart. I will not forget the Via Toledo [today Via Roma] any more than the view that one has of all the quarters of Naples. It is incomparable, to my eyes, the most beautiful city in the universe.... in Naples, at every turn of the street, you are surprised by a singular view of Mount Sant'Elmo, Posillipo, or Vesuvius...."

ABOVE: The small town that now bears the name Pompeii formerly was called Valle di Pompei. The name designates the little inhabited center that, from 1876 to 1891, grew up around the sanctuary of the Church of Our Lady of the Rosary, then under construction.

ABOVE: A fortress as well as a palace, the Angevin castle in Naples, usually known as the Castel Nuovo, was built in 1282 by Pierre d'Agincourt, who took the Château d'Angers as his model. During the Parthenopean Republic, a late-18th-century experiment in rebellion against the Bourbon monarchy, the castle would stand before Neapolitans as a grandiose reminder of the evils born of absolute power. RIGHT: At this little port—Borgo Marinaro —the Castel dell'Ovo projects into the sea like the prow of a ship. Its construction was begun under the Normans, then continued by the Angevins in 1274, under the direction of the architect Pierre de Chaulnes.

Until excavations began in 1748, Pompeii had lain buried for seventeen centuries under layers of lapilli and ash 4 meters deep. The ancient city once again reveals its houses, streets, and frescoes, as well as people and animals struck down on that fateful day in A.D. 79. However, thanks to this tragedy, which preserved the remains, we can read ancient history far better here than would otherwise have been possible. Certainly better than in Rome, where the temples and amphitheaters have suffered endless abuse.

The child of colonizers who arrived from Sybaris in the 7th century B.C., Paestum (originally Poseidonia) on the Bay of Salerno is a living lesson in the canons of Achaean architecture. In the center of the photograph stand the so-called Basilica and the Temple of Neptune, built of a gray travertine stone whose color turns to a rich, reddish shade when illuminated by the rays of the setting sun. The Forum and the Amphitheater demonstrate that, despite the comings and goings of four different peoples, from the Greek colonists to the Roman Empire, Paestum never lost its importance in the seaside world of the Sele Plain. The paintings discovered in 1968 in a nearby tomb, among them the famous *Diver* and *Banquet*, are the only known ancient Greek paintings in Italy.

THE ISLANDS AND THEIR PEOPLES

The island regions and the islands of the region—the subtle distinction between them must be understood by anyone wishing to fly over or survey Italy's wealth of insular assets. Sicily and Sardinia are island regions. Secret and mysterious, Sicily is heavily laden with history and tragedy, rich in ancient monuments and ruins, and ravishingly beautiful. Sardinia, the home of enigmatic monuments, lives essentially within herself, keeping intact both her traditions and her language, all three dialects of it. This island is less violent and volatile than her neighbor, also less extraverted. As for the islands of the region, small or large, there are 66 of them, all very unevenly distributed around the coasts. Even though said to be influenced by the mainland, they nonetheless boast of a certain individuality—one with its smoking volcano, another with its exiled Emperor, still others with grottoes of every kind or a philatelic museum unlike any other in the world.

Sicily constitutes an untidy accretion of an immense cultural heritage, age-old fame, and bloody dramas—repeated, odious, ongoing—that sometimes leave the contemporary visitor in a state of shock. Still, great poets and writers have expressed both profound love and genuine respect for Sicily. Why did Homer and Virgil find the island so fascinating, devoting to her a number of important pages in the *Odyssey* and the *Aeneid*? And Dante, what did he really mean when he referred to "the island of fire"? One thing certain is that Mount Etna made the Sicilian people at once haughty and apprehensive, accustomed as they became to seeing in that formidable, eternally fevered chimney the true thermometer of the ills afflicting the island. Its strange, tricuspid form allowed a geopolitical name, Sicilia, to be reconciled with the artistic name Trinacria, which signifies "Three Peaks." It was the Greeks who first called the island Sicily. Sometime during, probably, the 8th century B.C., they undertook major political and economic initiatives on several sides of the island, which then became known as Sikelia. However, coexistence with the Achaeans and the Dorians, who too were immigrants, eventually triggered savage conflicts in which the native population also became involved. Alternating periods of prosperity and war explain why the large cities of the period—Agrigento, Syracuse, and Catania—took turns suffering through eras of great commercial power and catastrophic defeat.

Then came the expansionist ambitions of Carthage, the African neighbor, which completely undercut the island's will to independence. After the first Punic War, in 246 B.C., Sicily became a Roman province, which brought the sole relatively tranquil millennium of her entire history. Finally, in 900, it was Islam that troubled the waters anew. Still, thanks to the learned civilization they brought, their disruptive arrival marked the beginning of an all-important epoch.

PAGES 164–165: Viewed from the air, this plain in the Foggia, or Capitinata, region of Apulia looks as if it had been produced by a painter rather than by farmers with their machines. The photograph could be a document reporting what came to be known in the 1970s as Earth or Land Art.

PAGES 166–167: The island of Mortorio off the coast of Sardinia is an unforgettable scene of jagged cliffs and small beaches washed by a turquoise and emerald sea.

LEFT: Gallinara (from the Italian *gallina* meaning "hen") owes its name to the wild fowl that once made their home on this round islet, whose surface measures less than 1 square kilometer. Situated opposite Albenga on the Ligurian Riviera (Riviera di Ponente), Gallinara is host to the ruins of a Benedictine monastery as well as to those of an Early Christian church.

Procida in Campania consists of four volcanic craters partially inundated by the sea. It is the wildest of the islands in the Bay of Naples. Hoping to attract tourists on their way to Capri or Ischia, Procida offers hospitality notable for its natural simplicity.

The beauty of the Sardinian landscape has inspired many writers, among them Auguste Boullier in 1864: "The panorama changes according to time and place, without ever, under that hot and pure sky, ceasing to fill the traveler with wonder....The sea, on which the moon casts its silvery reflections, touches the imagination with ideas of infinity, which remind man of everything that is greater than himself. The eye sees nothing but indistinct masses, and the soul, being no longer distracted by the spectacle of nature, withdraws into itself under the full light of its own thought or in the voluptuous half-light of its reveries." LEFT: The beach at Stintino on the northwest coast of Sardinia.

Then, following the Norman interlude, which endowed Sicily with genuine political relevance, Frederick II of Swabia appeared on the scene, bringing with him the splendors of the 13th century. Palermo recovered its brilliance, especially in matters of culture, and would long remain a magnificent and esteemed court. Now, however, the Angevins landed, giving rise to grave fiscal as well as political problems that, in 1282, ignited long-smoldering popular discontent. The famous "Sicilian vespers" began when several devout Sicilians, while leaving church after a service, rebelled against a group of French soldiers who insulted one of the ladies. Meanwhile, Pedro III of Aragon declared himself "protector" of Sicily, and the pendulum of power swung again. In 1415, the island became a vice-royalty, which wiped out what little political significance it still retained. In the course of subsequent centuries, the Spanish, the Austrians, and the Bourbons successively ruled over Sicily. Under their guardianship, the true character of the island came to the fore, as the Sicilians grew weary of domination from without and commenced bidding for their independence. They would not win it until 1860, when Garibaldi led the expedition of the *Mille*, a force of some one thousand volunteers whose liberation march through Sicily and the South constituted one of the most decisive and dramatic events of the Risorgimento, which produced modern, united Italy.

Sicily has made multiple contributions to art and literature. The staggering number of invasions and lasting or fleeting colonizations all fatally left their mark, sometimes with violence. The theater at Syracuse and the one at Taormina give grandiose witness to the Greek presence. The remarkable mosaics in the Roman villa at Piazza Armerina, near Enna, draw tens of thousands of tourists eager to experience the unique quality of this artistic treasure. Centuries later the Normans brought to architecture the extraordinary innovations of Romanesque France. From the union of Byzantine and Arab concepts were born the cruciform, marble-encrusted churches, among them the cathedrals of Palermo, Cefalù, and Monreale.

In painting—an art that flourished in Sicily around the turn of the 15th century—one is tempted to trace a long straight line between two major, albeit extremely distant points of reference: Antonello da Messina in the 15th century and Renato Guttuso in the 20th. The influence of Jan van Eyck's Flemish painting on Antonello shares much with the dramatic, descriptive realism of Guttuso, who took it upon himself to limn with full emotional power the everlasting tensions and conflicts of this land.

Literature as well became a passion. To transform Palermo into a leading intellectual center, Frederick II personally encouraged a revival of Sicilian poetry. Poets from all over Italy poured into Sicily, where, in an atmosphere worthy of a stadium, they took lively part in poetry contests attended by Frederick, his sons, and the high officials of the kingdom. The linguistic form of the period—the so-called "vulgar"

Palmaiola is a tiny island in the Tuscan archipelago. Today the lighthouse is the only evidence of human life.

idiom—was born of that spontaneity sparked by currents brought from afar. Several centuries later, Sicily witnessed the spread of the literary genre known as *verismo*, which, in the courageous work of Giovanni Vega, revealed the elements and humors of those two pillars of Sicilian society—the peasantry and the provincial bourgeoisie—perfectly embodiec in the Malavoglio family and the attorney Don Gesualdo. Pirandello carried the development further, with his perceptive analysis and exasperating pessimism, the latter nonetheless essential to his kind of theatrical voice.

The leading Sicilian cities—Palermo above all, but also Catania, Trapani, Enna, Caltanisetta, Agrigento, Ragusa, Messina, and Syracuse—are much too often forced to cope with a depressing reality—the Mafia. This devastatingly corrosive phenomenon has given the island its funereal reputation, which in turn gravely undermines the collective march towards social and economic progress. A well-known humorist, Giorgio Forattini, frequently represents Sicily in the guise of a crocodile's head that devours even as it weeps. Nevertheless, the big cities struggle to prevent the hypocritical head from becoming the fixed emblem of their land. Sicilians are a proud, passionate people, and there can be no doubt that one day soon justice will be meted out to those who have evaded it far too long.

The other large island is Sardinia, the four sides of whose rectangular shape align almost perfectly with both meridians and parallels. It has a typical island history. The first known human contribution came with the Phoenicians who settled there in the 9th century B.C. They were followed by the Carthaginians who, in 238 B.C., ceded Sardinia to Rome. The Roman Empire was in turn ousted in 456 by the Vandals, led by Genseric. The Byzantines following in their wake committed such widespread plunder that the local populations turned to the Church for a privileged intermediary in a campaign of strategic reorganization. Around the turn of the 11th century, Pisans and Genoese vigorously set about the task of driving out the Saracen invaders, only for the supposedly sincere alliance between the two maritime powers of Pisa and Genoa to present an opportunity for them to challenge one another for supremacy in Sardinia. Now Frederick Barbarossa appeared and, in return for a magnanimous distribution of money, made Sardinia a kingdom, whose governance he assigned first to Barisone II, supported by the Genoese, and then to the Republic of Pisa.

At the end of the 13th century, Sardinia found her protagonists in the Aragonese, whose opportunity surely arose in part from the island's own frequent bouts of political instability. Despite strong local opposition, the Spaniards continued in power until 1713, when, following the War of the Spanish Succession, Sardinia passed into the hands of Austria. However, on 2 September 1720, at the conclusion of accords between France and Great Britain, Victor

Alicudi in the Aeolian archipelago. Although modest in size—its area is barely 5 square kilometers—the ancient volcanic island of Ericusa, or modern Alicudi, yields crops that are far from ordinary: capers, carob beans, and "Barbary figs" (prickly pears).

Mount Etna. The gaping maws of the volcano no longer emit from the bowels of the earth anything more alarming than a vaporous plume that dissolves in the atmosphere. Around the volcano's base, the land is incredibly fertile; here, the orange, lemon, and olive groves, like the vineyards, yield abundant harvests.

The little port of Cetara, on the Amalfi coast, attracts tourists during eight months of the year, regaling them with the famous local plums and fish soups. The graceful bay reminds visitors of how easy it once was for Saracen pirates to make their raids. But after the fast-moving vessels entered the bay, their sailors often settled there.

Amadeus II of Savoy took possession of Sardinia in a land swap of a sort dictated by geopolitics since time immemorial. Until 1870, when Italy finally achieved unification, the political life of the island underwent the usual settling process in the aftermath of earthquakes. During the reign of King Charles Albert, the enormous potential of the mining sector encouraged the rapid development of exploitation companies. Huge drainage and reclamation projects characterized the end of the 19th century. At the beginning of the 20th century, Sardinians renewed their determination to be free of mainland politics, and independence movements proliferated. These did not last long, since triumphant Fascism, with few scruples, made short work of isolationist ambitions. After the Second World War, however, Sardinia's Action Party revived and, in alliance with other democratic elements, worked towards making the island "an autonomous region by special statute."

In certain respects, Sardinia resembles her Sicilian cousin, but not in the overall realm of art and culture, where the singularity of the archaeological remains is most evident. This is particularly true of the *nuraghi*, the conically shaped fortress-houses, fashioned from huge, superposed blocks of stone, that date from the 2nd millennium B.C. It also applies to the bronzes found on the island, extraordinary witnesses to the dawn of Sardinian history. This was long before Byzantine and Romanesque art would flower here, evidence of the first to be found in the Basilica of Saints Cosmas and Damian and the second in the Virgin of Bonacattu sanctuary. In the island's agriculture-dominated south, sheep-rearing thrives anew as an ongoing, unbreakable tradition. But a different face of Sardinia has become familiar for the past several decades, one that exploits her natural beauty in order to promote the tourist industry. It has the earmarks of a new desecration, a new merciless colonization. An atavistic smile—resigned and perhaps typical—immunizes the Sardinians and keeps them happily apart from such pollution, both cultural and environmental.

When it comes to the smaller Italian islands, one must guard against underestimating the reality of their historical importance. Today as yesterday, tourism is the motor force of the local economy. Sicily and Sardinia may now be too subject to bureaucratic controls to satisfy the adventurous spirit of the sailor who likes to land on whatever rock may seem inviting. But elsewhere this kind of free spirit can find a wealth of choice among Italy's islands. Sixty-six of them provide enough scope to satisfy both the romantic and the rough side of the relationship between man and sea. Fundamentally diverse natural settings, customs as various as the regions they depend upon, explosions of human riches and folklore, some of the islands also constitute tesserae in the grand mosaic of history.

Scoglio dello Sparviero in Tuscany. This "sparrow-hawk" reef, 2 kilometers off the coast of Punta Ala, is favored by Florentines as a place for Sunday picnics.

There is no ignoring the historic importance of Elba, a one-time possession of the Maritime Republic of Pisa and the assigned place of confinement for a celebrated exile. Napoleon spent almost a year there. Ambitious and cultivated, Elba's principal towns—Portoferraio, Porto Azzurro, Marina di Campo—have, over time, acquired everything essential to hospitality of the finest quality.

A rugged half-moon—that is Ponza, the Isle of Rome. It can boast of having been host to human inhabitants as early as the Neolithic period, well before the Volsci and the Romans settled there. Like Elba, Ponza became a land of exile, from the time of the Carbonari in the early 19th century to the Fascist era.

For many, Capri is the island of first preference, a pearl set in the Bay of Naples, situated at some antipodal extreme from the precarious, socioeconomic state of the surrounding territory. Its role, which remains magnetic, was built up over the millennia, by the Roman Emperors Augustus and Tiberius, the Normans and the Swabians, and finally, in 1860. its assimilation into the Kingdom of Italy. This rich past and long history have permitted all manner of subtle minds to express themselves, to write and live in an exquisite setting—Joseph Conrad, Oscar Wilde, Graham Greene, André Gide, Axel Munthe, Arturo Toscanini, Curzio Malaparte, and Gracie Fields. All understood how to partake of and promote the natural beauty, strong humanity, and extravagance of Capri. Thus we find Maxime Du Camp writing in 1862: "Once we had passed through the entrance to the celebrated Grotto Azzurro, we discovered ourselves in pure enchantment. Everything is blue—the sea, the boat, the rocks. It is a turquoise palace erected upon a sapphire lake. It is the most beautiful natural wonder I have ever seen."

Other islands, other marvels, large or small—Ischia, Procida, the Aeolian Islands, the Egadi, Ustica, Giglio, Cetara, Giannutri—are all quite different, and yet they all make a coherent human milieu. The accidents of geography apparently left them dotted around the peninsula in random fashion. Solid and patient, with their reefs wide open, they are content to be judged as such. Although isolated by nature, they nonetheless float on currents of sympathy that run from one to the other.

Of the several islands and their relationships with the countries of the Mediterranean, Fernand Braudel has written: "For this Mediterranean world, the history of the islands, like certain enlarged images, offers the most illuminating account. It does more to explain how each Mediterranean province could preserve its own irreducible originality, such a potent regional flavor, in the midst of an extraordinary mingling of races, religions, customs, and civilizations."

The island of Giglio in the Tuscan archipelago. Also known as "Lily Island," Giglio bears traces of human presence from prehistoric times to the era of the Etruscans. The Romans also recognized the island's strategic value. The other islands of the Tuscan archipelago became known for a variety of reasons, one as a penal colony, another as a nature preserve. Meanwhile, Alexandre Dumas immortalized the name of Monte-Cristo.

Palermo Cathedral from the northeast. The people of Palermo, the Sicilian capital, are passionately devoted to their patron saint, Rosalia. Daughter of a Palermitan noble, the Duke of Roses, the Sicilian virgin lived in retirement in a cave on Mount Pellegrino. In the 17th century, the relics of Saint Rosalia were borne in procession as prayers were offered for deliverance from the plague then decimating the city's population. The epidemic did indeed cease, after which Palermitans raised a statue to the Saint.

Cradled between Cape Zafferano and Mount Pellegrino, Palermo sits majestically in the plain called the Conca d'Oro or "Golden Shell." Originally, the city, a Phoenician port from the 8th to the 6th century B.C., was called Panormus. After the Carthaginians fortified the site, the Romans seized it. Under Byzantine control for three centuries, beginning in 535, Palermo then fell to the Arabs. As the capital of the Sicilian emirate, the city entered a period of unparalleled splendor, becoming the bridge between Europe and the Near East. The Swabian emperors transformed Palermo into a cultural center, but the Angevins ruined the city. Much later, it came under the rule of Emperor Charles V. Next, in 1713, it was the House of Savoy that took control, then Austria in 1720, followed by the Bourbons, whom Garibaldi expelled in 1860. Finally, in 1947, Palermo became the capital of an autonomous Sicily. Although seriously damaged during the Second World War, the city has lost none of its seductive charms.

Catania is one of Sicily's most important cities. Densely populated, the port is a commercial center where a well-managed economy combines with intelligent exploitation of the natural beauty to save Catania from many of the ills that afflict other parts of Sicily. Historically, however, Catania has not been immune to the doleful fate shared by all of the island's urban centers. In addition, the city has several times been destroyed by an erupting Mount Etna.

The regular layout of Catania, designed by the architect Vaccarini, dates from the 18th century. The famous Via Etnea runs across the city from end to end, skirting the east side of the gardens named for Vincenzo Bellini—the composer of *Norma* and *La Sonnambula*, born here in 1801— and leading north towards Mount Etna. In the 13th century, Frederick II of Hohenstaufen had the austere Ursino Castle built on the waterfront, but lava from Etna's eruption in 1669 left it completely land-bound.

Taormina in Sicily. ABOVE: Built into a hillside overlooking the sea, the ancient theater of Taormina was originally planned in the 3rd century B.C., in the reign of Hieron I. It would undergo extensive alterations in the course of the Roman era. The orchestra, in particular, was transformed into an arena surrounded by a wall designed to protect spectators at gladiatorial contests. RIGHT: Founded in the 5th century B.C., Taormina still retains monuments and ruins dating from Greco-Roman antiquity, as well as having churches and palaces that rival one another in their grace and charm. Piazzas, terraces, and gardens on the steep hillside all provide serene views over the sea, towards Etna, and south to Acireale on the coast.

PRECEDING PAGES:
In Sicily, plains are
rare, and barren parts
adjoin regions of
extraordinary fertility,
such as the Conca
d'Oro or "Golden
Shell." The land was
long monopolized by
great latifundium lords
who practiced extensive
cereal farming. Today,
a more diversified
agriculture is given over
largely to the
production of grapes,
olives, almonds, citrus

fruits, and cotton.
ABOVE AND RIGHT:
Favignana, the capital
of the Egadi Isles.
Situated northwest of
Sicily, facing Trapani,
Favignana is as flat as
a hand and pitted with
long-abandoned tuff
quarries. Unsuspected,
delightful pockets of
green mark the
orchards that now
flourish there. Tuna
fishing, with nets or
harpoons, has the air of
a solemn ritual.

The island now called Vulcano was known in antiquity as Hiera' Thermassa or Terasia. According to legend, Aeolus, god of the winds, lived here. Vulcano, in the Aeolian Islands, is of volcanic origin, as the name implies, and still active, a fact that is not without its appeal for travelers in search of a thrill. The slopes are rugged and the craters impressive, while the warm-water springs and sulphurous muds are used in the treatment of various ailments.

The Aeolian Islands include Stromboli, with its volcano almost always emitting a plume of smoke. The volcano erupts at frequent intervals, sending lava and white-hot stones tumbling and crashing into a crevasse called the *sciara del fuoco* ("hothouse of fire"). The white cubic houses are Arabian in type. From the vineyards of this wild island come the delicate Malvasia wine or "malmsey."

The Isle of Capri, off the Bay of Naples in Campania. ABOVE: A pair of tooth-like rocks formed by the action of wind and water, the *faraglioni* ("rocky islands") create a gateway leading to the best sites for bathing on the south shore of the island: Tragara, Unghia Marina, and Marina Piccola. RIGHT: Capri, with an area of only 10 square kilometers, has had an extraordinary history, much of it associated with pleasurable living. Strolls through the island's semi-tropical vegetation are sheer enchantment. As menacing as the open jaws of a lion, the *Salto di Tibero* ("Tiberius Leap"), with its 300-meter-high cliff, recalls the dark rumors, reported by Suetonius and Tacitus, concerning the cruel punishment that the Emperor Tiberius inflicted upon his victims, who were said to have been cast into the sea from the top of this rock.

ABOVE: Porto Cervo in Sardinia. The first signs of the new local architecture were seen at Porto Cervo in 1962, when the ambitious holiday/residential scheme of the Consorzio Costa Smeralda got underway.

LEFT: Lipari, the largest of the Aeolian Islands. Here, volcanic slopes descend straight into the sea on every side, while cooled by constant brezes circulating around Mount Chirica, 602 meters in height. The rather curious white areas, which could be taken for snow fields, are actually quarries from which pumice stone is extracted. The Norman Cathedral in the town of Lipari dates from 1084, and the Aeolian Museum was once the episcopal palace.

It would not do to regard the island of Ventotene as a mere annex of Ponza. Indeed, Ventotene richly deserves its title of "pearl" of the Pontine Islands, and its past history is just as full as that of its better-known neighbor. The two islands share the same Neolithic origins, and both have served as places of exile. Like Ponza, Ventotene is heir to valuable Roman remains.

The younger sister of Ponza, the island of Palmarola also belongs to the Pontine archipelago. The *grotelle* are evidence of human presence here from remote times. In habitations carved out of the volcanic rock, traces have been found of primitive people who gathered wood and obsidian. Now a nature preserve, Palmarola is almost always closed to mass tourism. Landing places are restricted by the rugged mountain terrain, with sheer drops into the sea, such as the Suvace reef and the rocky islet called Mezzogiorno.

Ponza was first colonized by the Latins, after which the Romans made it a bastion for defense during the Punic wars. Under the Empire, the nobility chose it as an exclusive resort. Later, Ponza also became a place of exile, as recently as the 19th century, during the Risorgimento, for the supporters of Mazzini, and also in the 20th century, for victims of the Fascist regime. Still, history has left the island's natural beauty unscathed.

Ponza is a volcanic island, with groups of houses forming amphitheater-like enclaves ranged about small ports along the steep coastline. The Romans treated Ponza as a kind of extension of the capital city. Although today mainly involved with tourism, the islanders have not lost sight of their land's potential. Agriculture, now dormant, may eventually be a source of crops and employment once again.

On Procida, off the coast of Campania, the houses of fishermen and wine growers have domes, arcades, terraces, and walls painted white, yellow, ochre, or pink. Here, Lamartine found safe haven, following a storm at sea, and met Graziella, the daughter of poor fisher folk who fell in love with the young poet. The affair ended in death for Graziella, but for Lamartine it was a moving idyll, which he evoked in a novel as well as in one of his most beautiful poems, "Harmonies."

Procida supports a population that is the densest in the whole of Italy. In past centuries, this island witnessed the passage of Etruscans, Tyrrhenians, Greeks, and Romans. To continue and maintain local maritime traditions, a shipbuilding school is active in the island's ports, one of which, Corricella, betrays a style remarkably like that seen on Capri.

The Isle of Elba, also known as the "isle of seahorses," is—like Sardinia, Corsica, and the Balearic Islands— a remnant of the lost continent, Tyrrhenida. In this view, the capital Portoferraio is seen surrounded by its splendid bay. A strategic site on Italy's third largest island, the city was defended by the forts of Falcone, Linguella, and Stella. As well as seahorses, tuna and anchovies are plentiful in the local waters.

A view of Portoferraio, which still reflects the ideas of its founder, Cosimo de' Medici, who laid the first stone in the 15th century. Napoleon, during his six-month exile on Elba, lodged in the Villa dei Moulini. Apart from its capital, the island has seven small towns and a major geographical feature, Mount Capanne, which looms above a massif rich in iron ore. Exploited by the Etruscans as early as the 6th century B.C., the open-cast mines remain the primary asset in the island's industrial economy.

LEFT: Mortorio. Despite its less than enticing name, which means "sad" or "dull," this island has nonetheless become a magnet for summer residents, mostly foreign, seeking "isolation vibrant with life."

ABOVE: Costa Smeralda in Sardinia. The aerial view seen here does justice to the feeling of intimate isolation that characterizes this part of the Sardinian coast, where places like Porto Cervo, Porto Rotondo, the Bay of Marinella, and the Bay of Volpe provide magical settings for those in search of tranquil paradise. Since 1962, a longing for perfect harmony between the beauties of nature and discreet, man-made structures has generated this lovely flower of Mediterranean tourism.

HISTORY

Arlacchi, P. *Mafia, Peasants and Great Estates: Society in Traditional Calabria* (J. Steinberg, tr.). Cambridge and N.Y., 1983.

Beales, D. *The Risorgimento and the Unification of Italy*. London and N.Y., 1982.

Braudel, F. *The Mediterranean and the Mediterranean World in the Age of Philip II* (S. Reynolds, tr.), 2 vols. London and N.Y., 1977.

Burckhardt, J. *Civilization of the Renaissance in Italy*. London and N.Y., 1990 (reprint).

Etienne, R. *Pompeii: The Day a City Died*. London and N.Y., 1992.

Ferrill, A. *The Fall of the Roman Empire*. London, 1981; paperback ed., 1990.

Finley, M.I. *Ancient Sicily*. London, 1979.

Guicciardini, F. *The History of Italy* (S. Alexander, tr.). Princeton, 1984.

Guichonnet, P. *Histoire de l'Italie*. Paris, 1989.

Hale, J.R. (ed) *Encyclopaedia of the Italian Renaissance*. London, 1988; reprinted 1992.

Hughes, S. *The Rise and Fall of Modern Italy*. 1983 (reprint of 1967 ed.).

Jannot, J.R. *À La Recherche des Étrusques*. Rennes, 1987.

Livy. *Rome and Italy*. London and N.Y., 1983 (paperback).

Machiavelli, N. *Florentine Histories* (L. Banfield and H. Mansfield, Jr., trs.). Princeton, 1988.

Moatti, C. *The Search for Ancient Rome*. London and N.Y., 1993.

Norwich, J.J. (ed) *The Italian World*. London and N.Y., 1983.

Romano, S. *Histoire de l'Italie du Risorgimento à nos jours*. Paris, 1977.

Villari, L. *Italian Life*. 1976.

TOPOGRAPHY

Bohm, D. *Venice*. London, 1992.

Grazzini, G. *Tuscany from the Air*. London, 1991.

TRAVEL ACCOUNTS

Beckford, W. *Dreams, Waking Thoughts and Incidents*. 1783.

——. *Italy: with Sketches of Spain and Portugal*. 1834.

Benjamin, W. *Reflections: Essays, Aphorisms, Autobiographical Writings*. N.Y., 1986.

Berenson, B. *The Passionate Sightseer*. London and N.Y., 1960 (paperback ed. 1988).

Block, A. *Poèmes et lettres d'Italie*. Paris, 1988.

Brosse, C. de. *Lettres d'Italie*. 1986 (reprint).

——. *Lettres sur l'état de la ville souterraine d'Herculée et sur les causes de son ensevelissement sous les ruines du Vésuve*. Paris, 1974 (reprint).

Chateaubriand, R. *Voyage en Italie*. Geneva, 1969 (reprint).

Dumesnil, A.J. *Voyageurs français en Italie depuis le XVIe siècle jusqu'à nos jours*. Paris, 1985.

Fernandez, D. *Le Promeneur amoureux*. Paris, 1980.

Goethe, J.W. von. *Italian Journey* (W.H. Auden and E. Meyer, trs.). London and N.Y., 1982.

Harder, H. *Le Président de Brosses et le voyage en Italie au XVIIIe siècle*. Geneva, 1981.

Hare, Augustus. *Augustus Hare in Italy*. 1988 (reprint).

James, H. *Italian Hours*. 1987 (reprint).

Stendhal. *Voyage en Italie*. Paris, 1973 (reprint).

——. *Rome, Naples et Florence*. Paris, 1987 (reprint).

Taine, H. *Voyage en Italie*. Paris, 1990 (reprint).

Tuzet, H. *Voyageurs français en Sicile au temps du romantisme (1802-1848)*. Paris, 1945.

LITERATURE

Lamartine, A. de. *Graziella*. Paris, 1979.

Leopardi, G. *Essays, Dialogues, and Thoughts* (B. Dobell, ed.; J. Thomson, tr.). 1979 (reprint of 1905 ed.).

——. *Poems and Prose* (A. Flores, ed.). 1987 (reprint of 1966 ed.).

Michelangelo. *The Complete Poems of Michelangelo* (A. Sidney, tr.). Athens, Ohio, 1991.

Montesquieu, C. de. *Considérations sur les causes de la grandeur des Romains et de leur décadence*. Paris, 1990 (reprint).

Schifano, J.N. *Désir d'Italie*. Paris, 1990.

Sciascia, L. *Pirandello et la Sicile*. Paris, 1989.

Shelley, P.B. *The Complete Works of Percy Bysshe Shelley* (R. and P. Ingpen, eds.). London and N.Y., 1965.

Titus Livius. *The 'History of Rome' of Livy* (A. De Selincourt, tr.). Harmondsworth, 1960ff.

ART AND ARCHITECTURE

Acton, H. *The Villas of Tuscany*. London, 1990.

Argan, G.C. *Brunelleschi*. Paris, 1991.

——. *The Renaissance City*. N.Y., 1969.

Chastel, A. *A Chronicle of Italian Renaissance Painting* (P. and L. Murray, trs.). London and Ithaca, N.Y., 1984.

Hartt, F. *History of Italian Renaissance Art: Painting, Sculpture, Architecture*, rev. London and N.Y., 1987.

Murray, P. *The Architecture of the Italian Renaissance*. London, 1986 (reprinted 1992).

Vasari, G. *Lives of the Artists* (G. Bull, tr.), 2 vols. London and N.Y., 1988.

Venturi, L. *La Peinture italienne*. Geneva, 1952.

Wöfflin, H. *Renaissance and Baroque* (K. Smith, tr.). London and Ithaca, N.Y., 1967.

Zeri, F. *Le Mythe visuel de l'Italie*. Paris, 1986.

Pisa. Close to the east end of the Cathedral, fashioned of marbles
in alternating colors and completed in 1118, the Leaning Tower dominates the
surrounding area. Shifting ground? Defective foundations? Masterly ruse
on the part of an architect eager to display his virtuosity? Very likely it will never
be known for certain why the tower leans, but Galileo was not
slow to take advantage of its tilt to make experiments
while studying the laws of gravity.

Pages 204–205: An 18th-century map of Italy (Explorer).

WILLIAM STOUT
ARCHITECTURAL
BOOKS

804 Montgomery Street
San Francisco, California
94133 USA

Telephone 415/391 6757

publisher Rizzoli

title ITALY FROM THE AIR

author Lefèvre

ISBN 140·X

paper   cloth   date